Underwater Ocean Coloring Book

By Herbert Toben

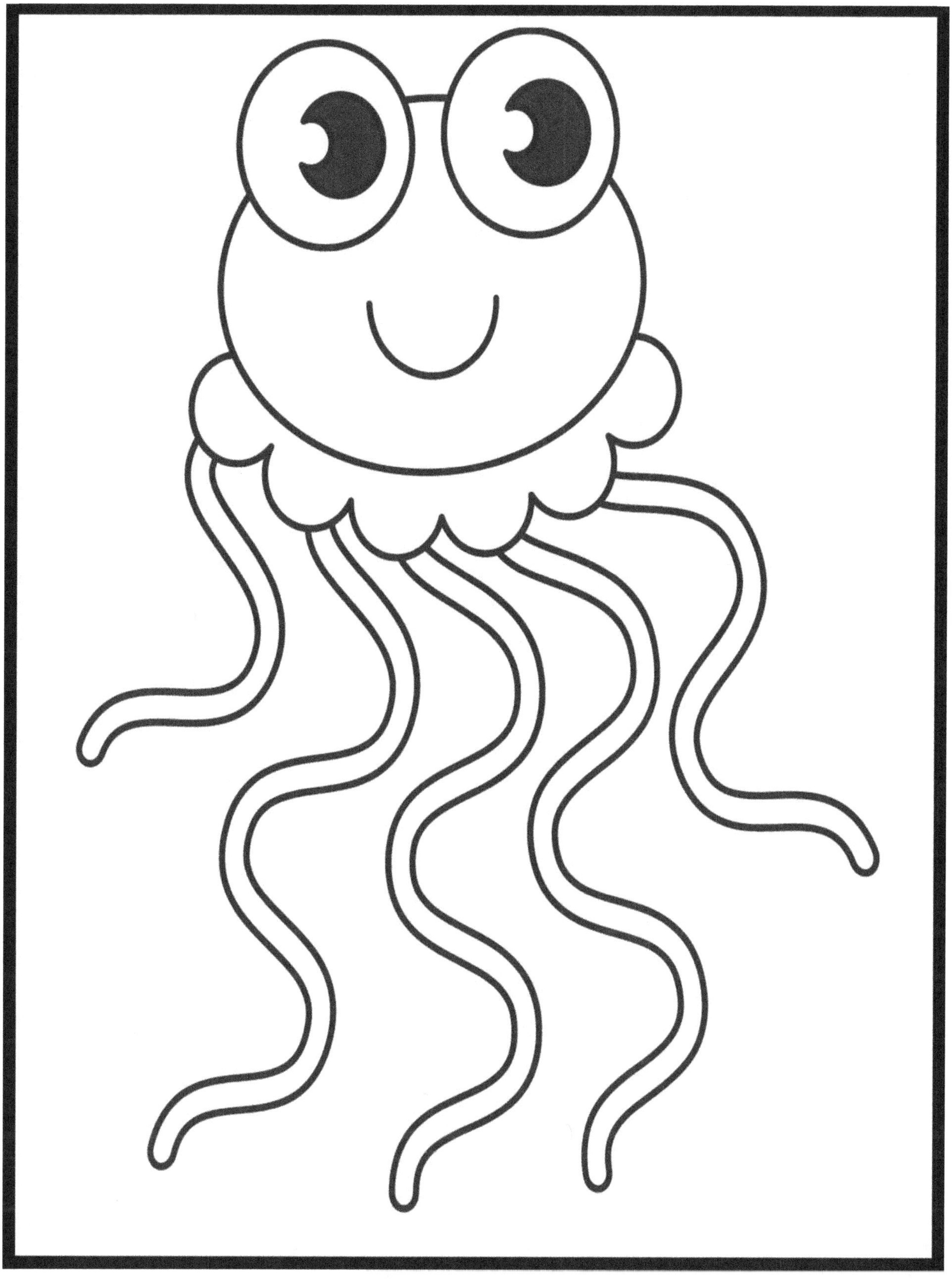

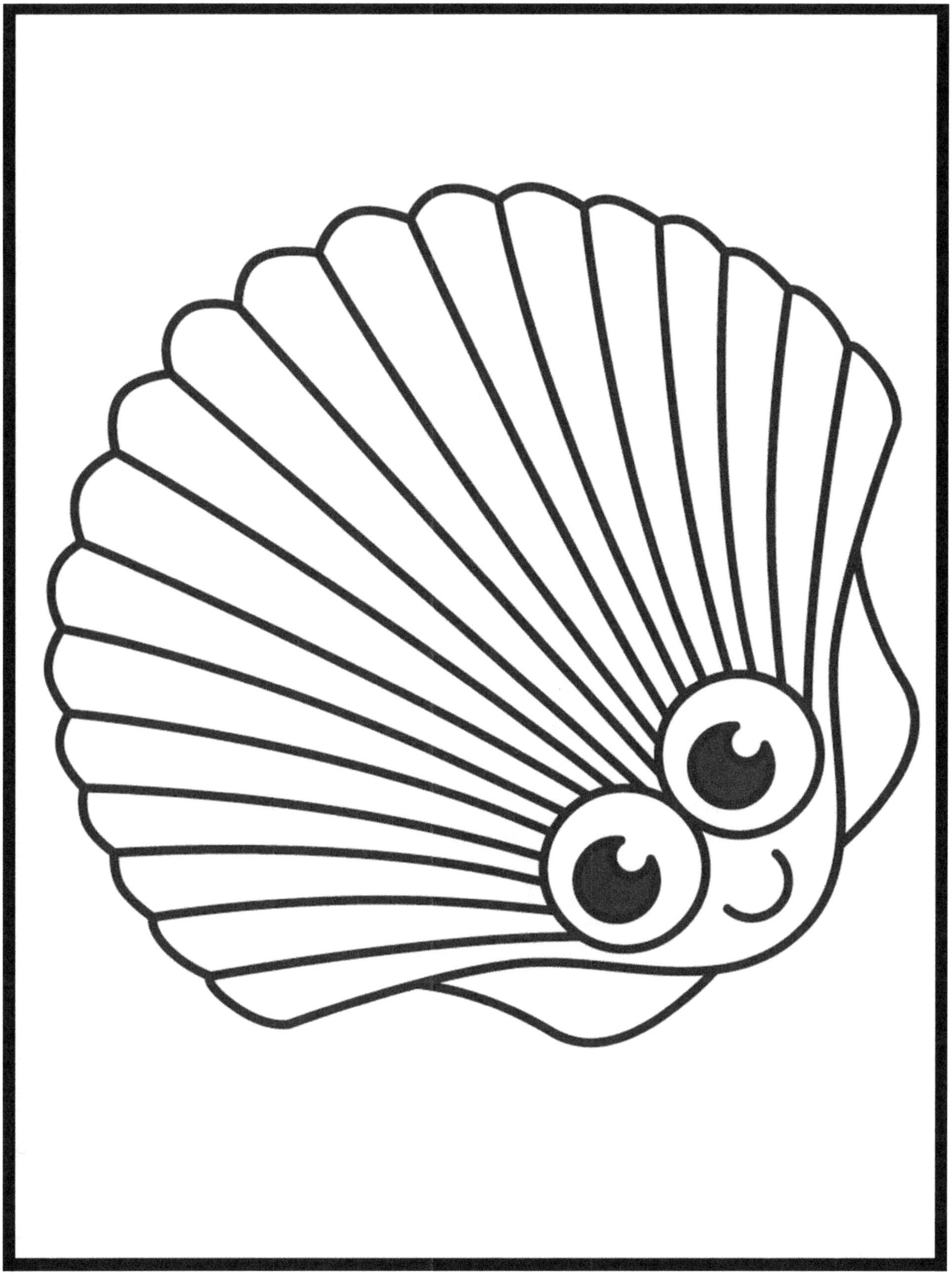

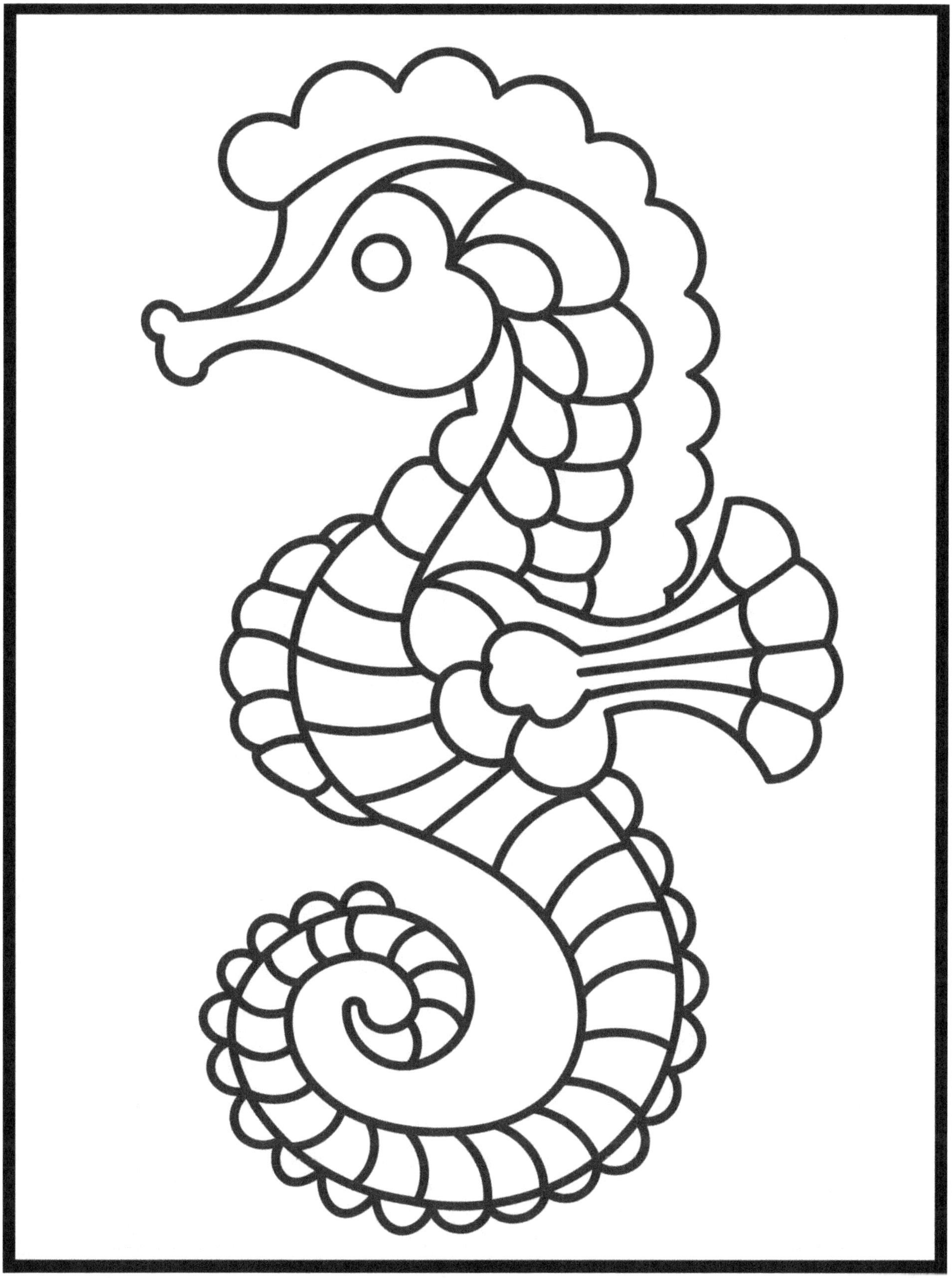

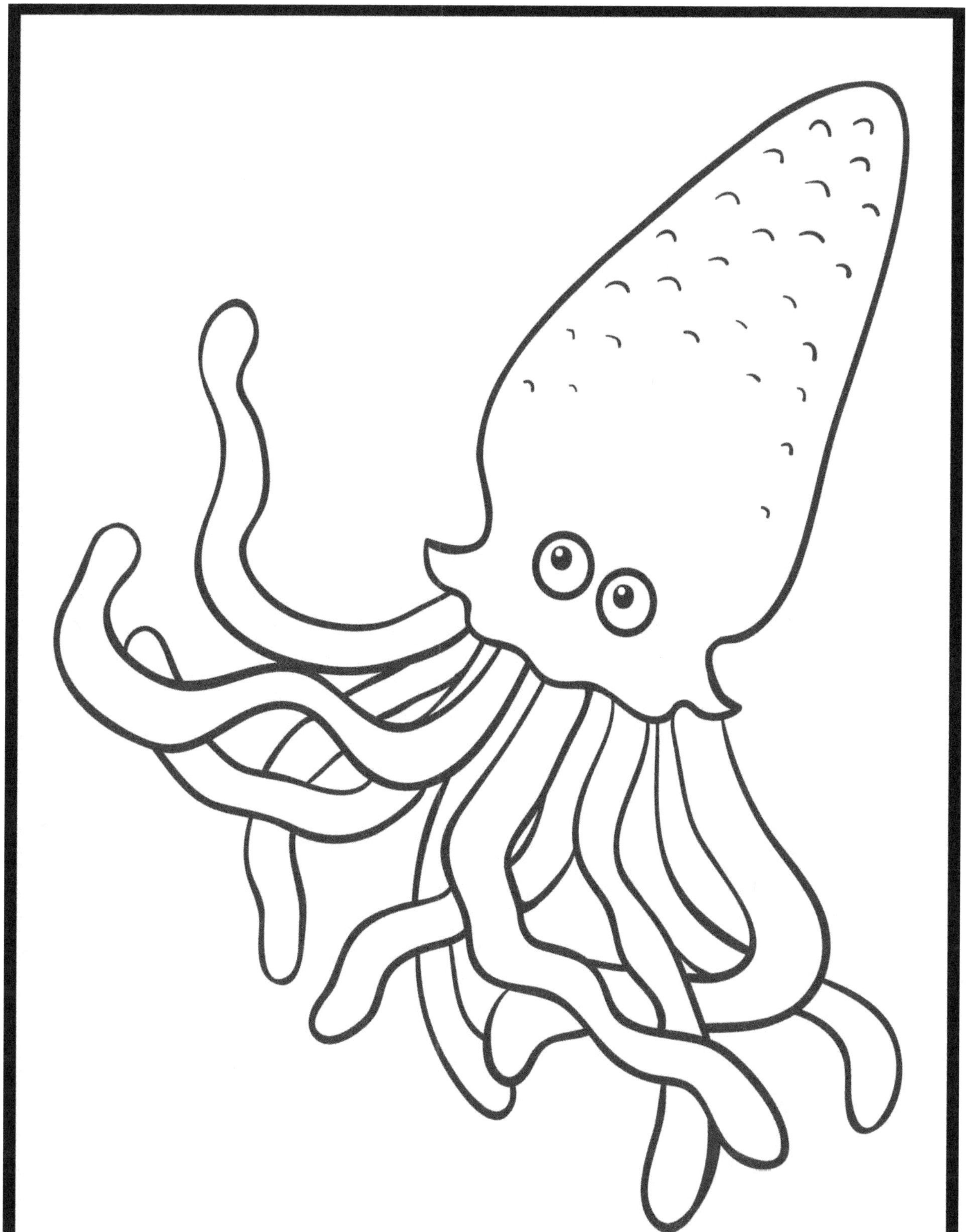

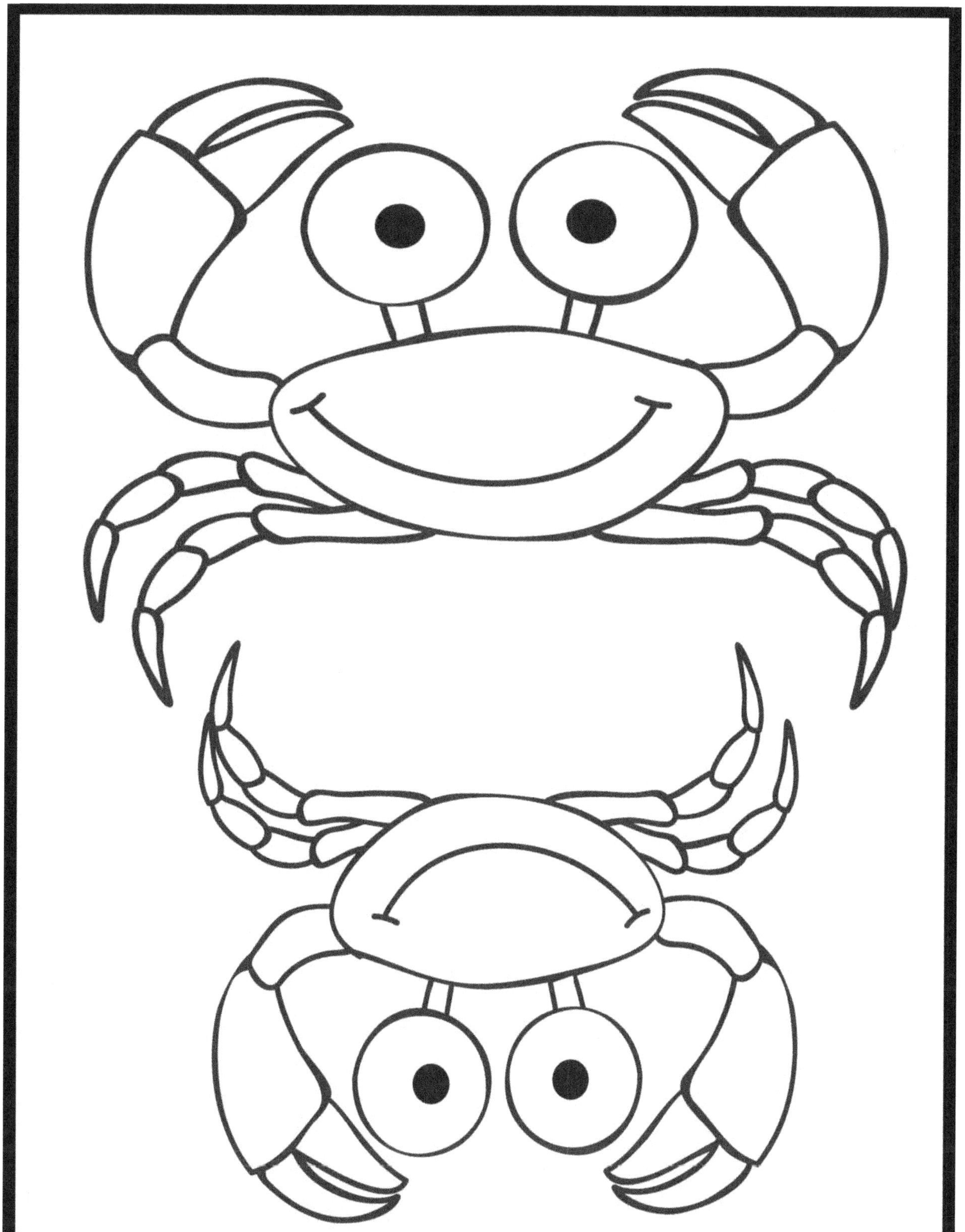

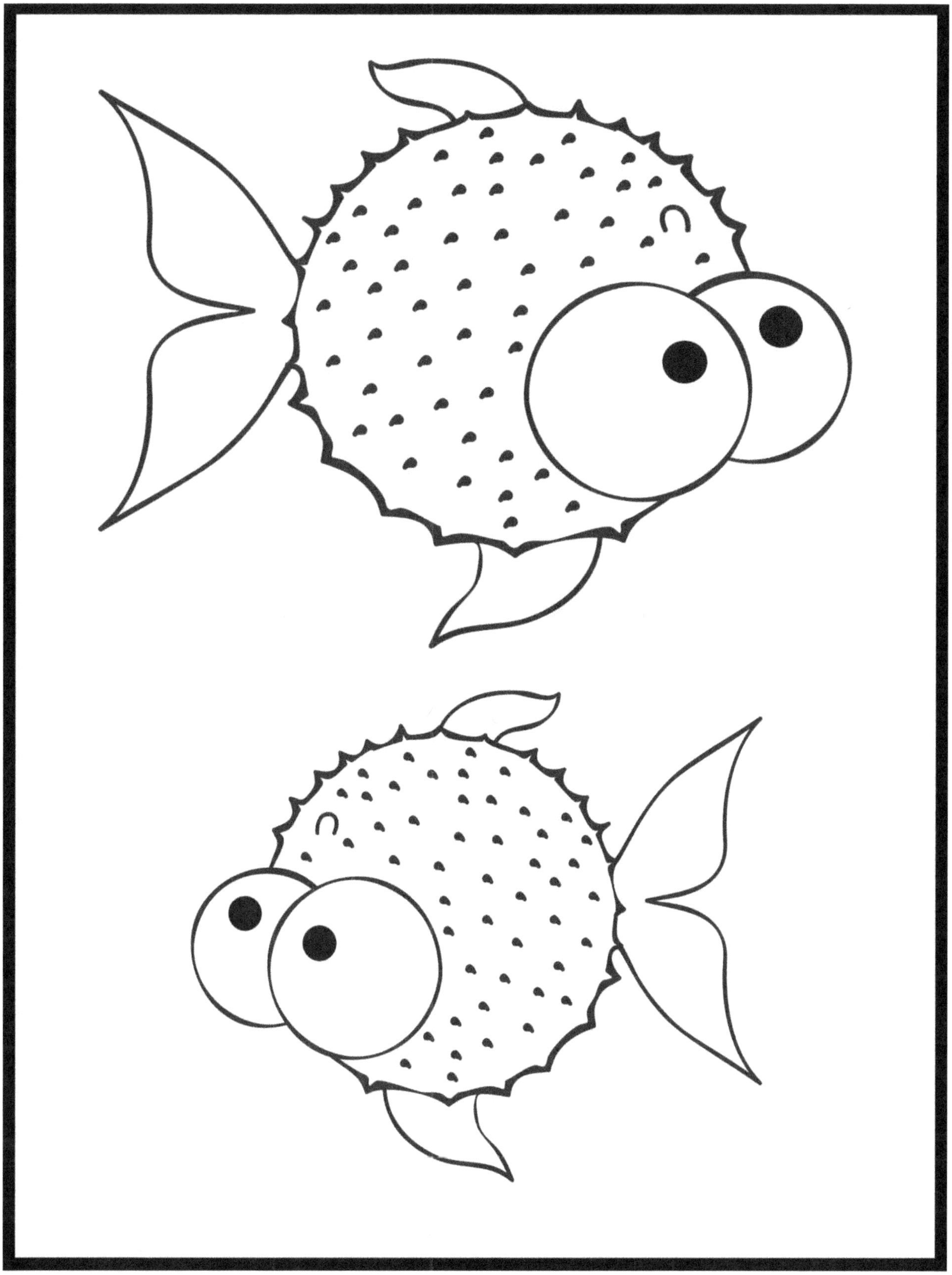

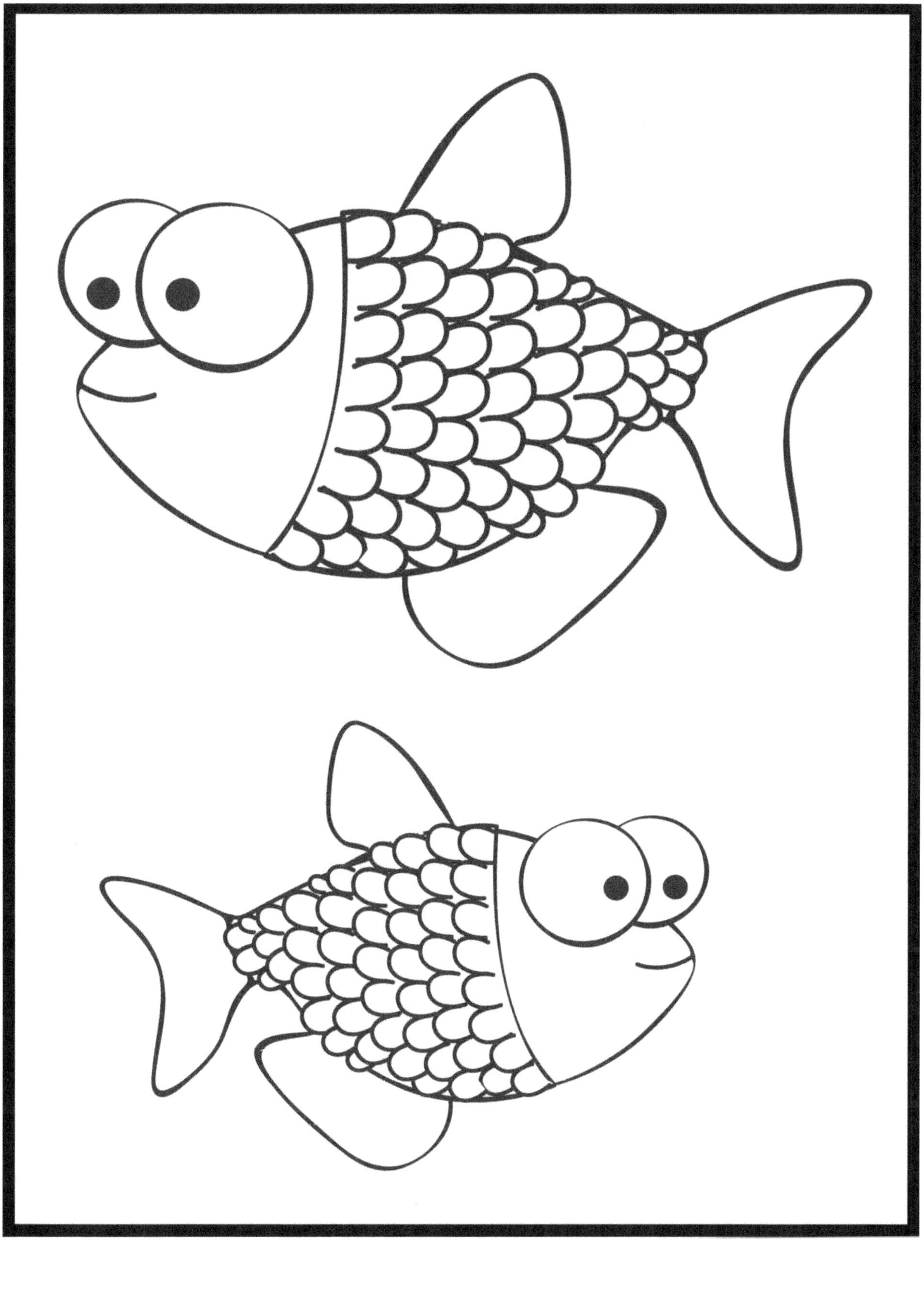

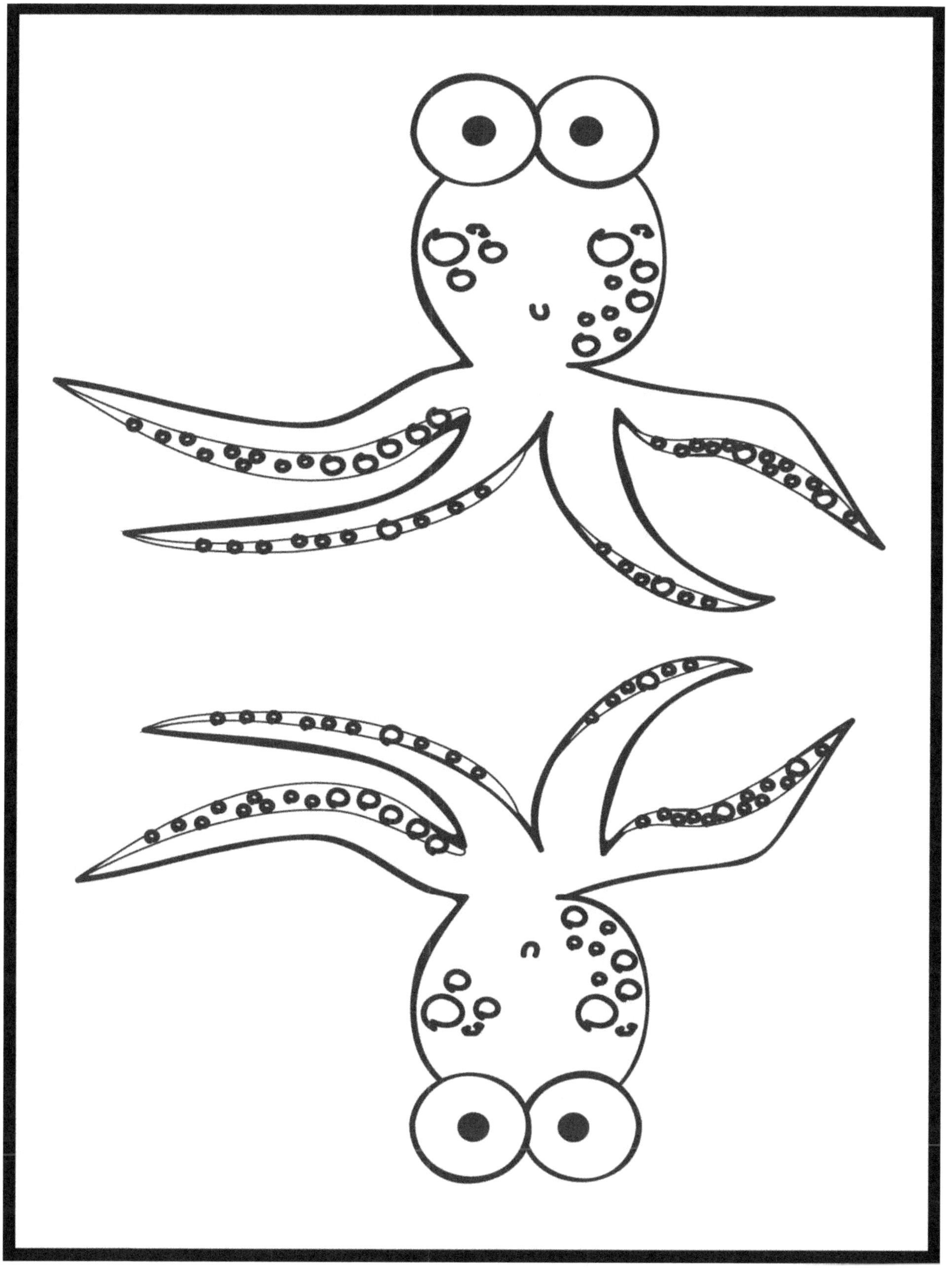

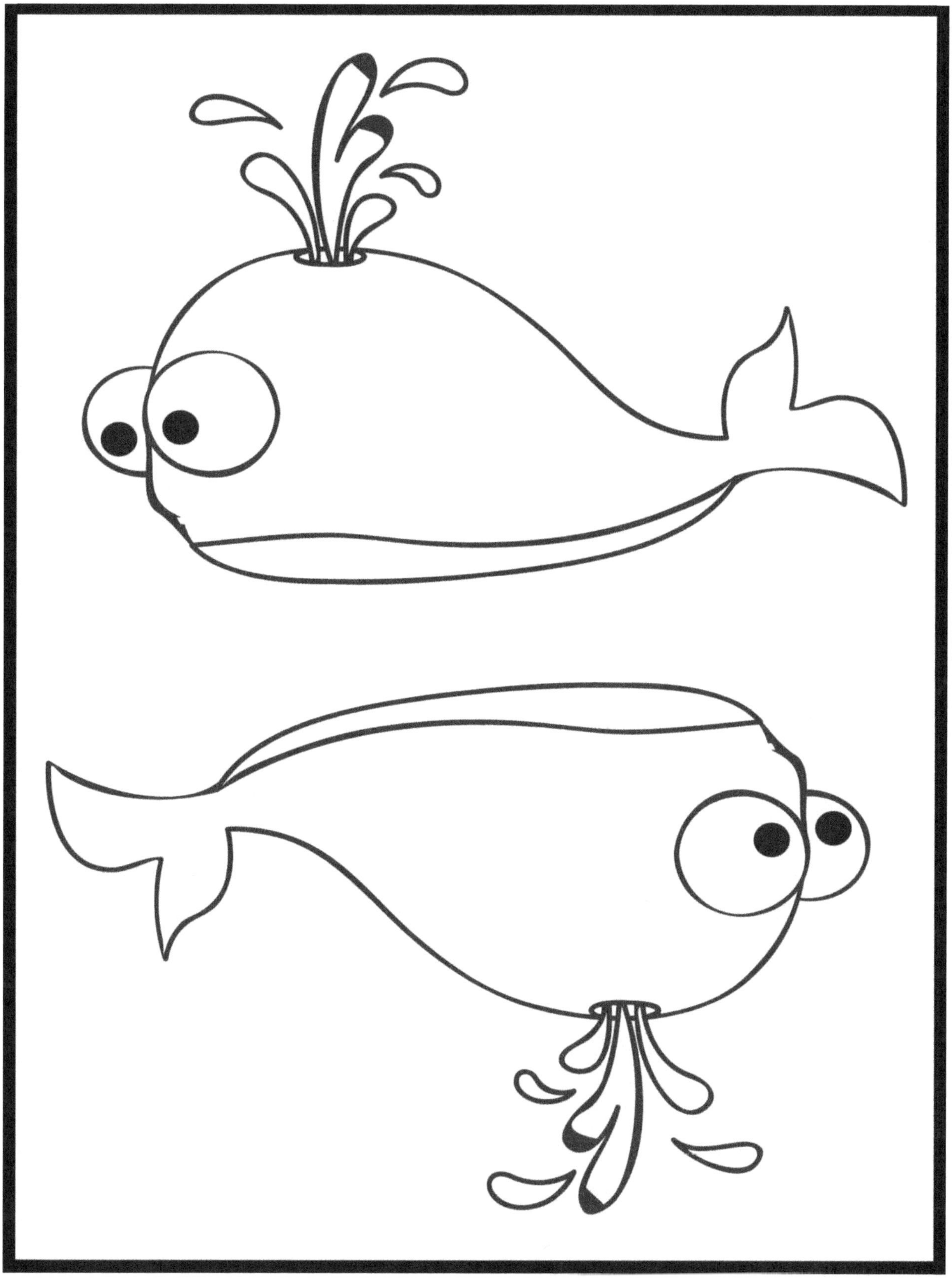

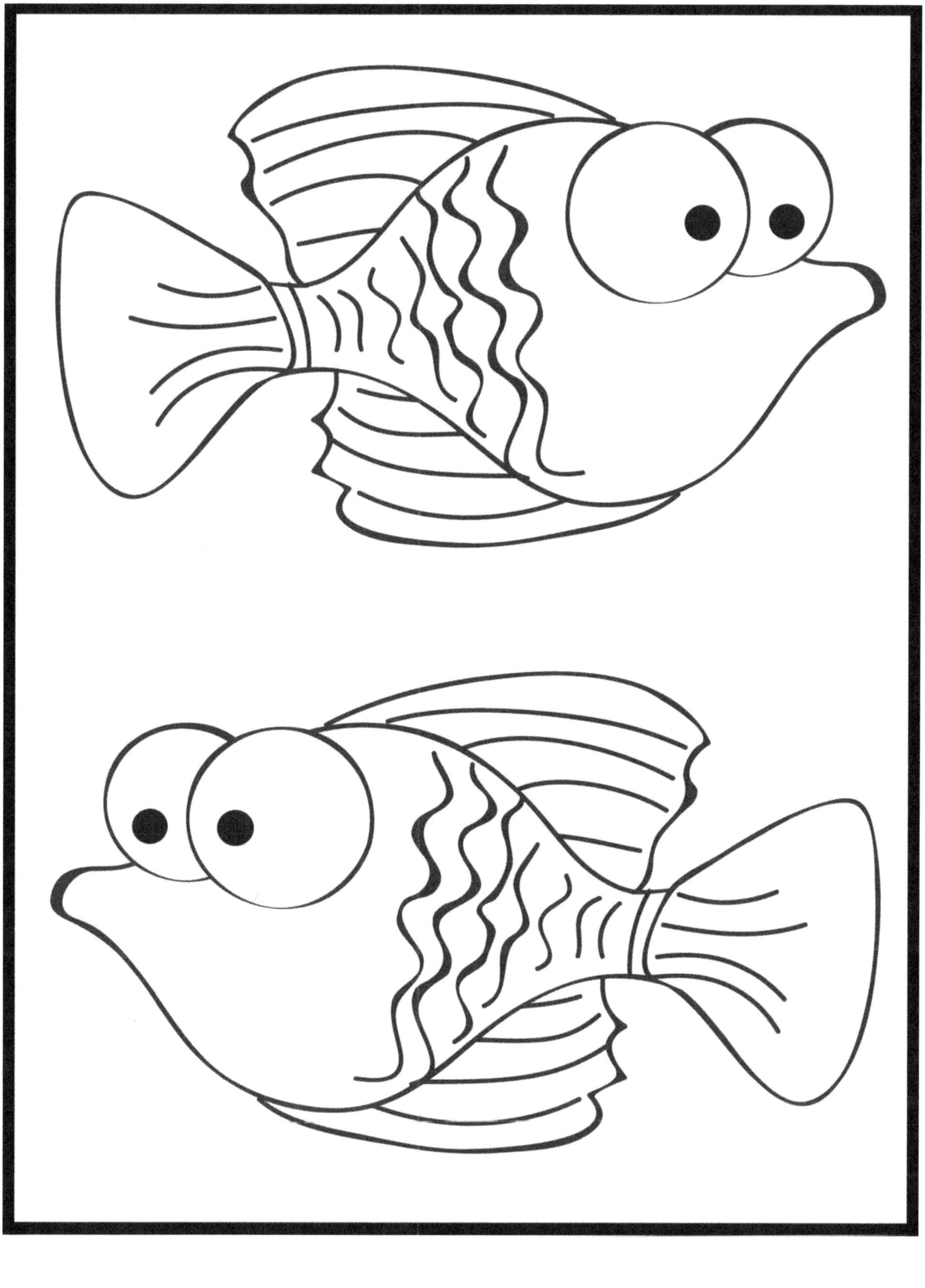

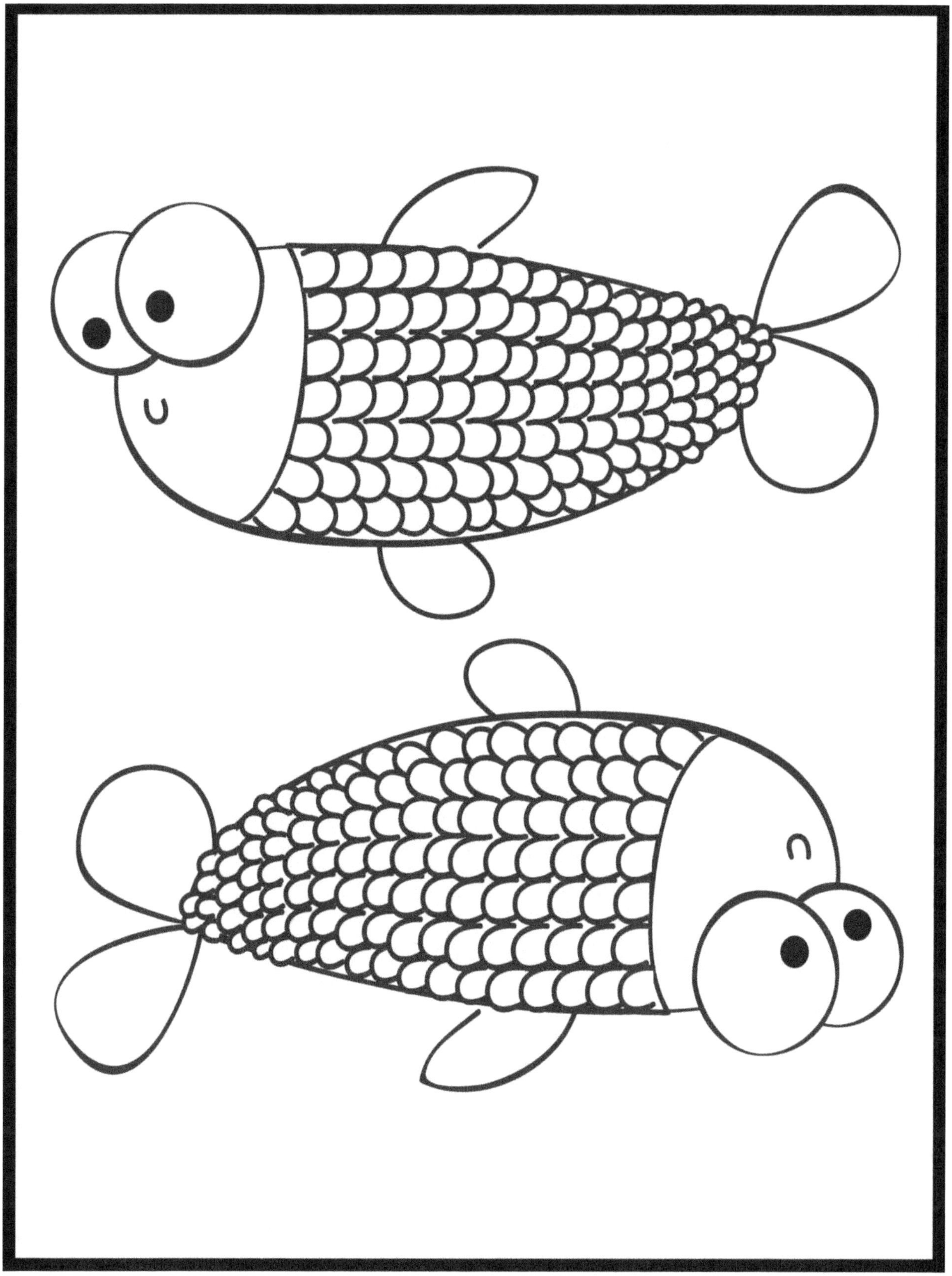

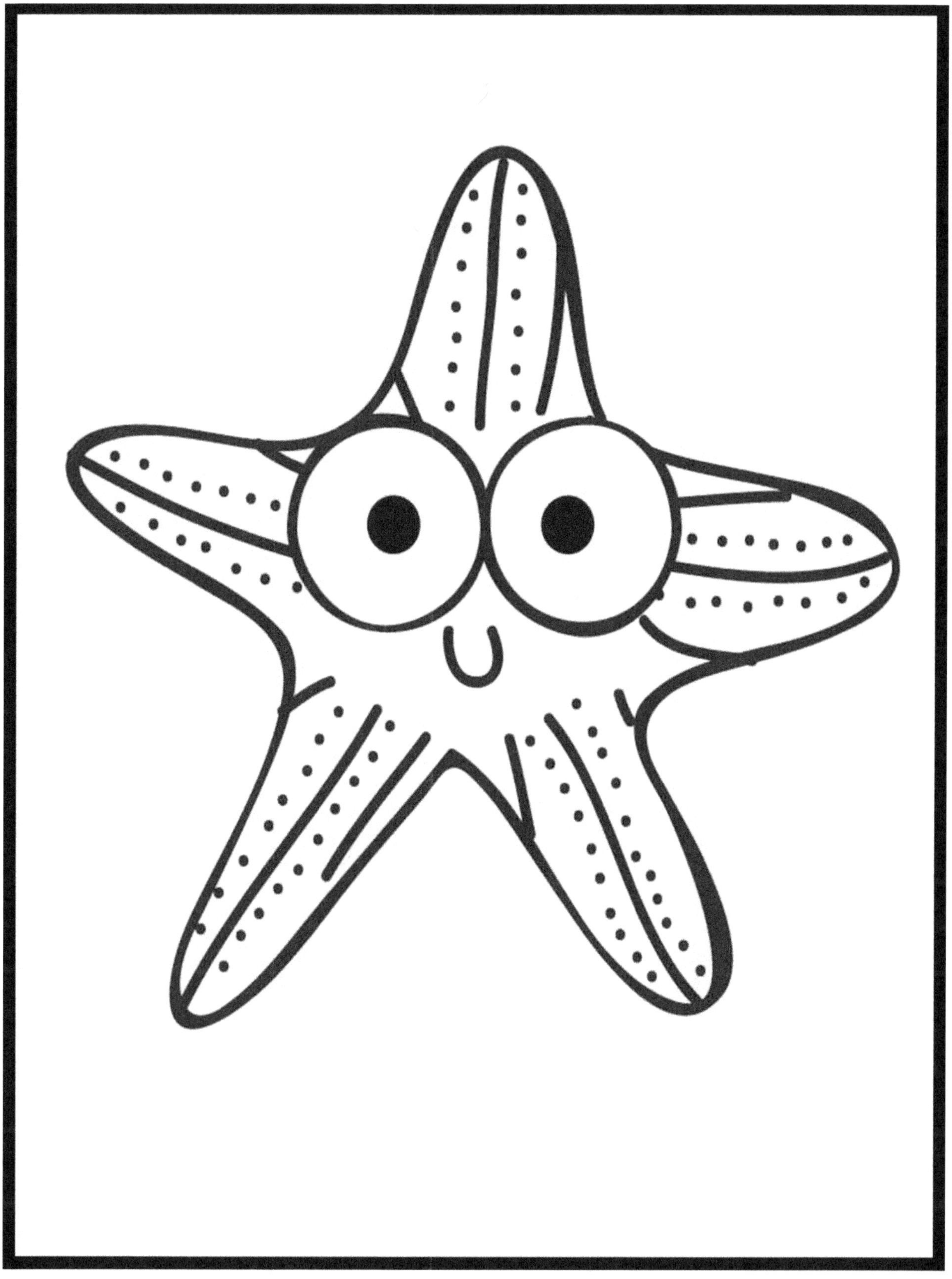

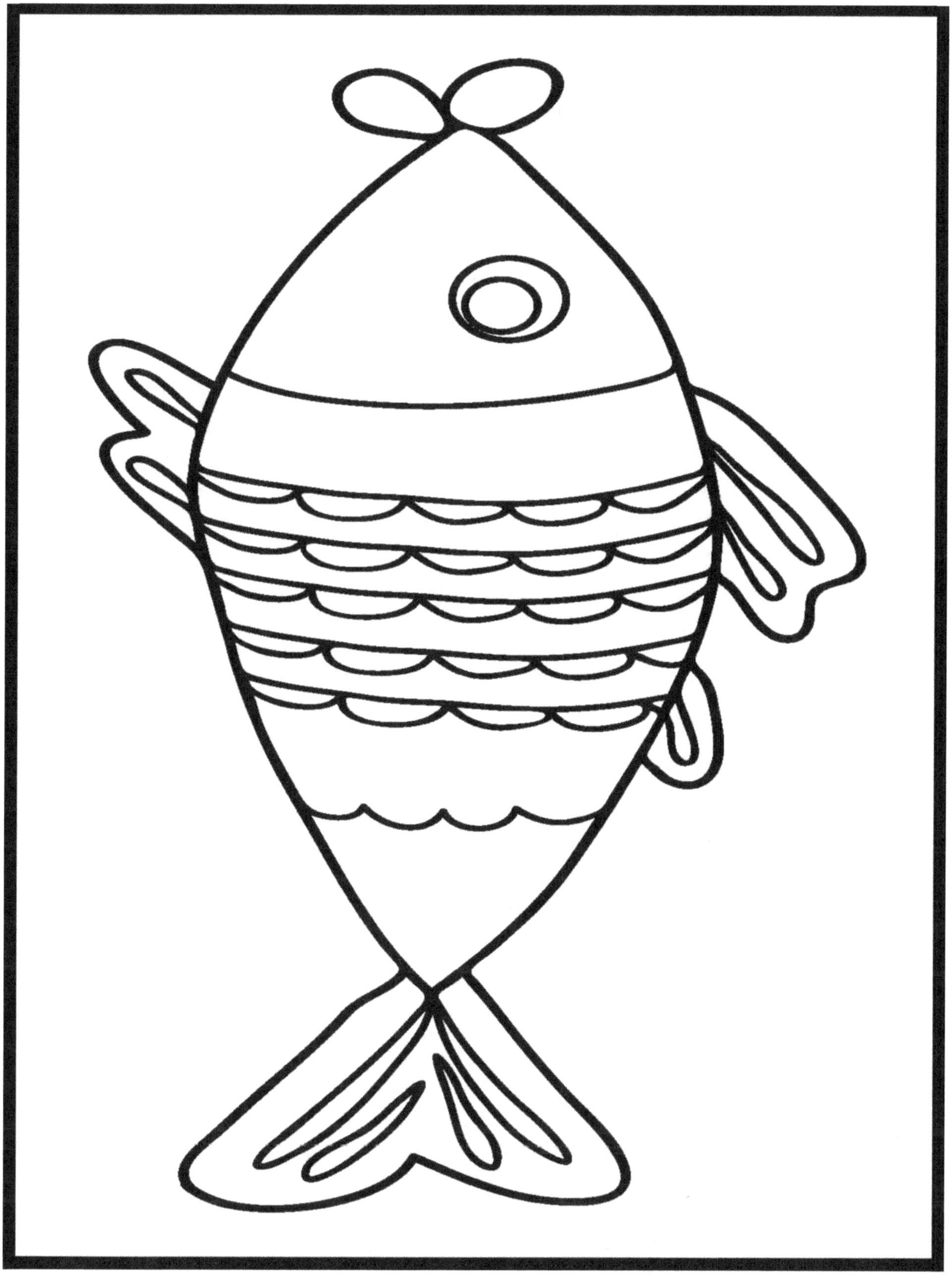

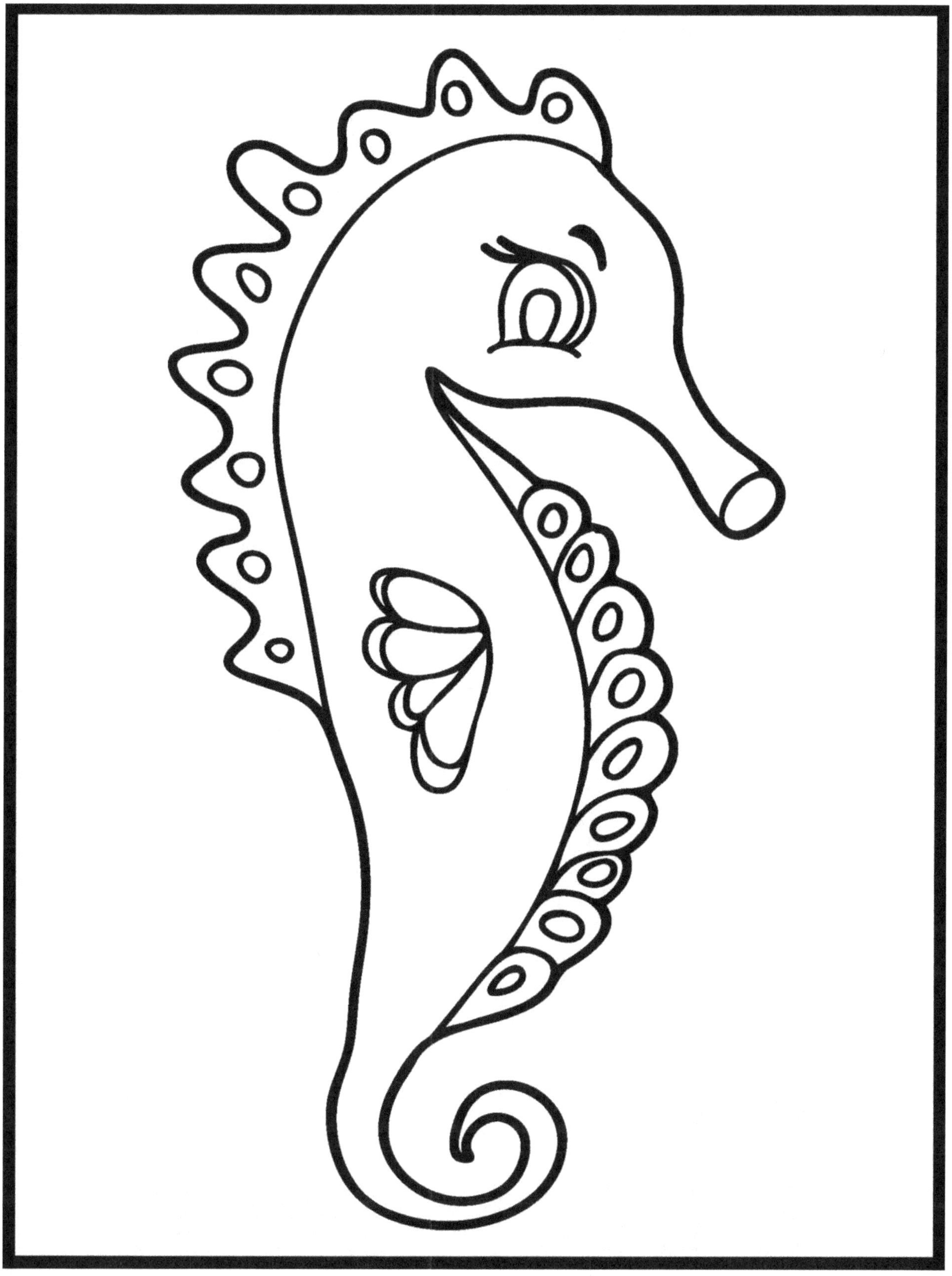

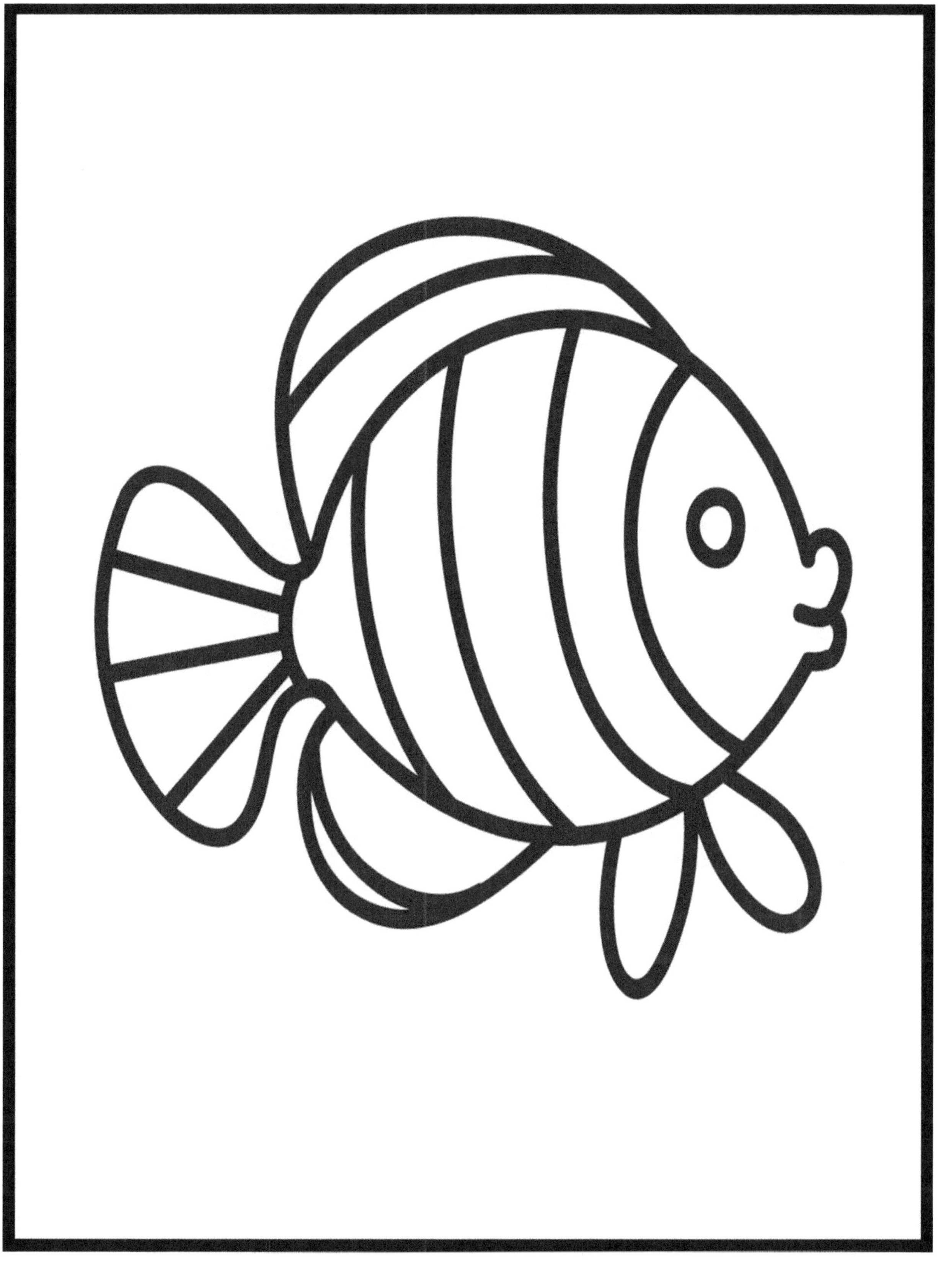

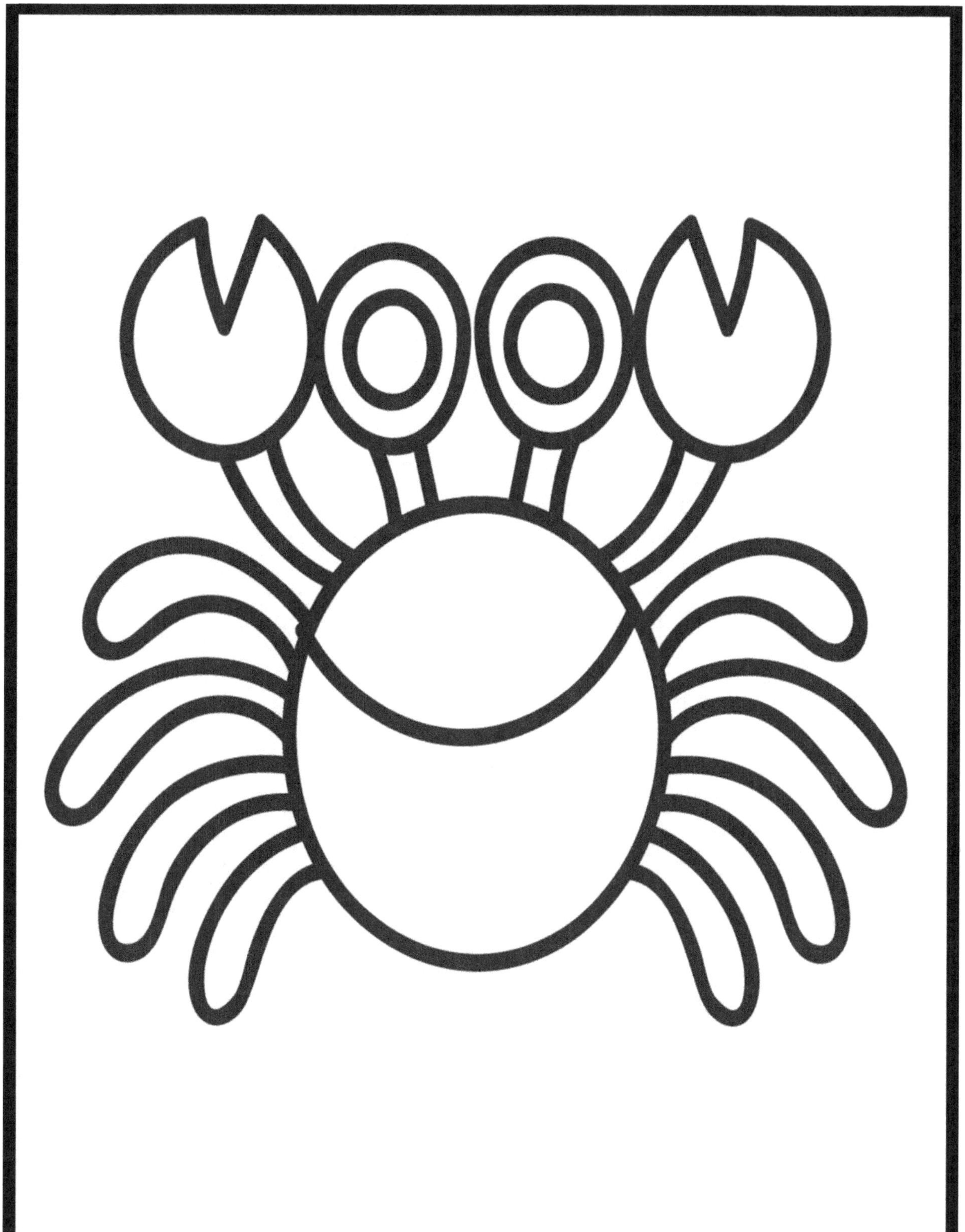

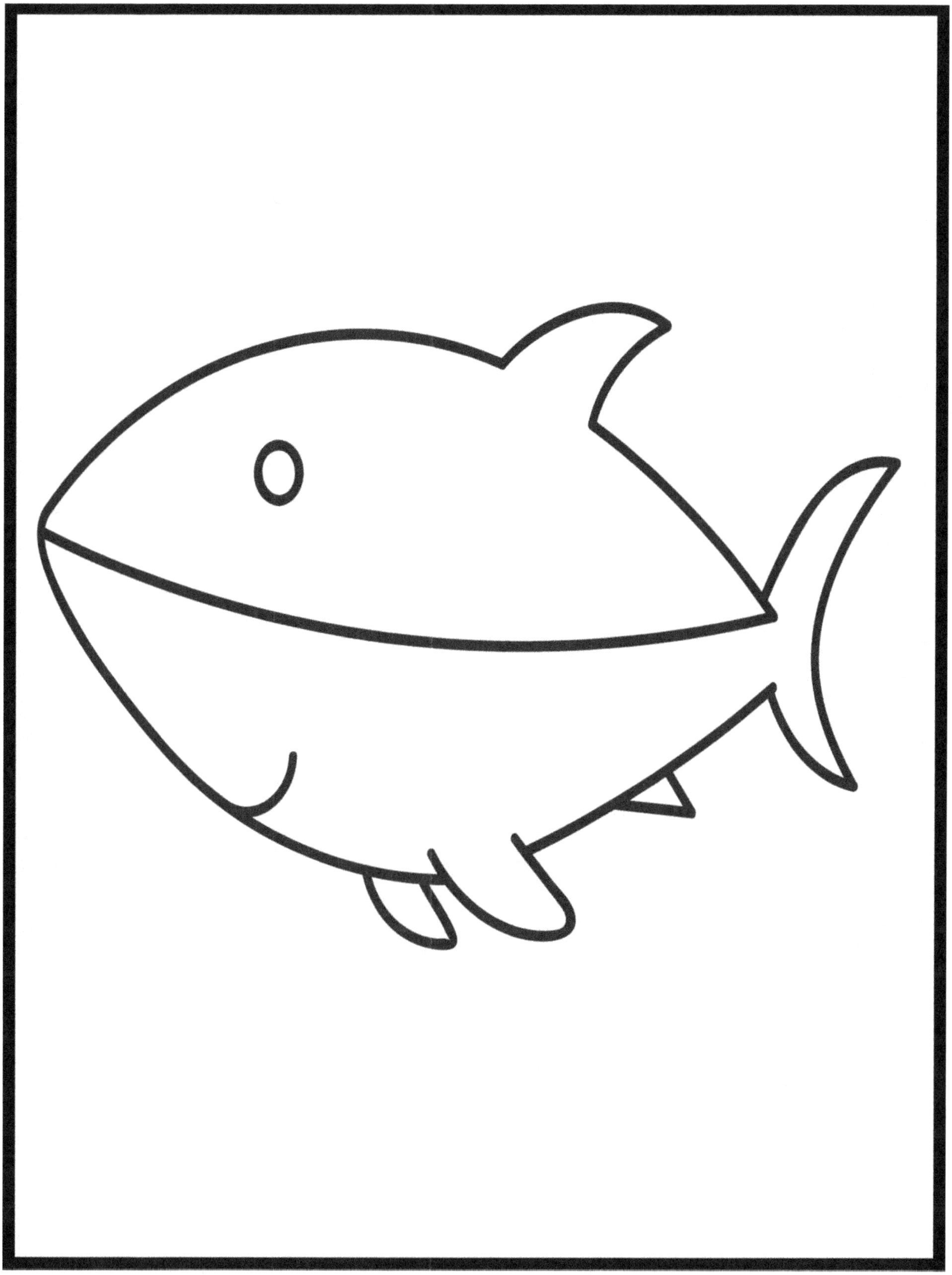

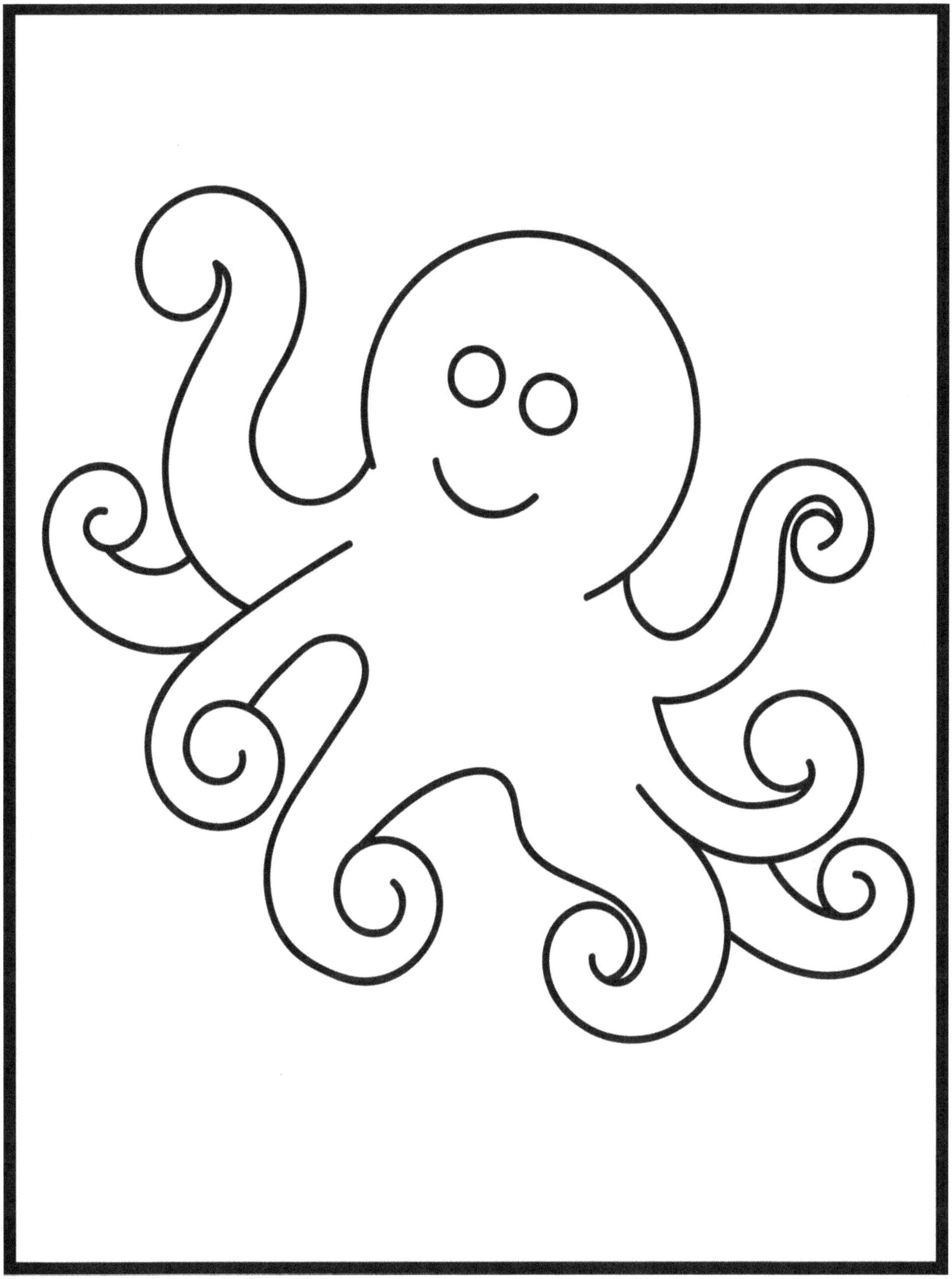

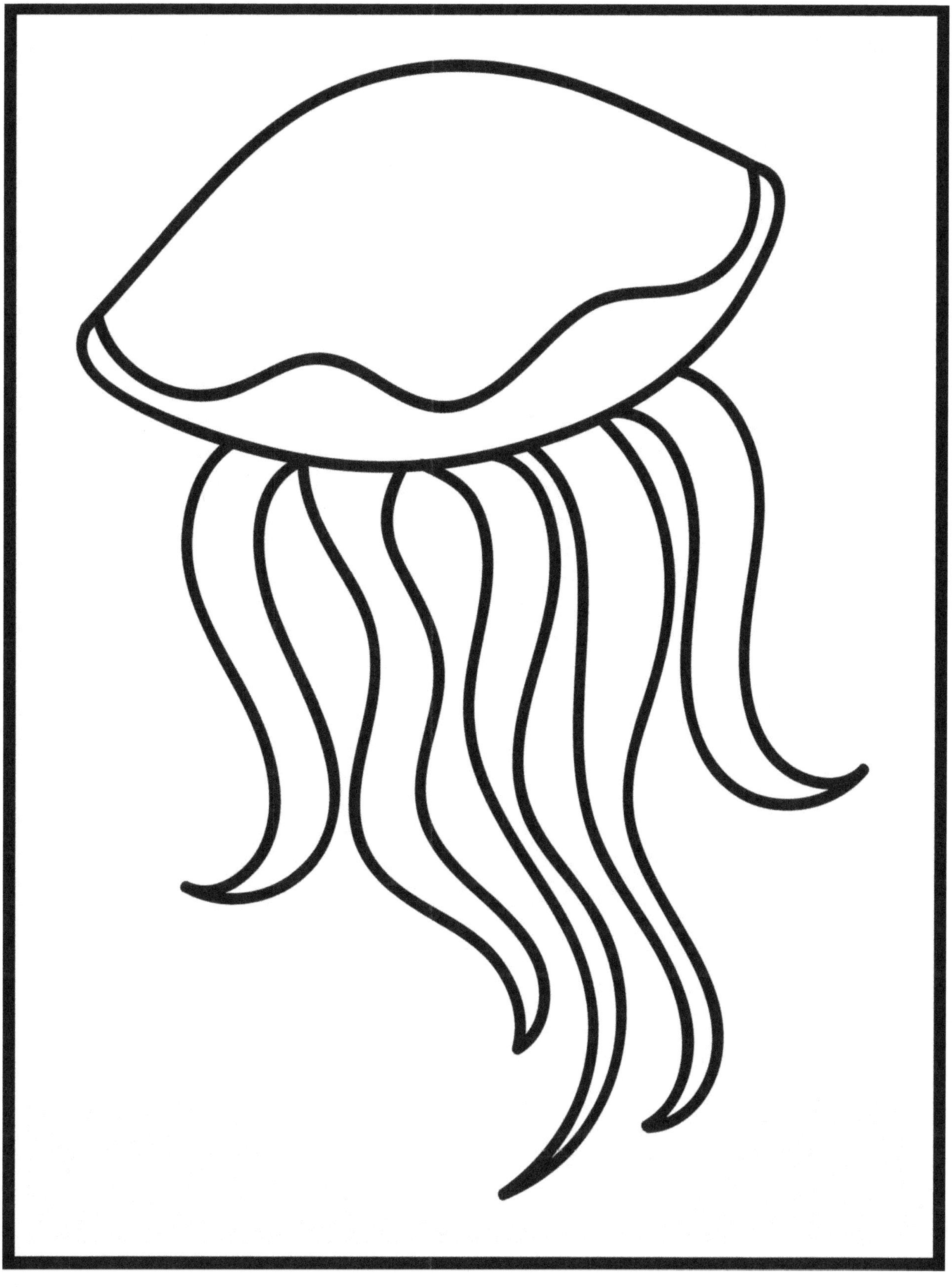

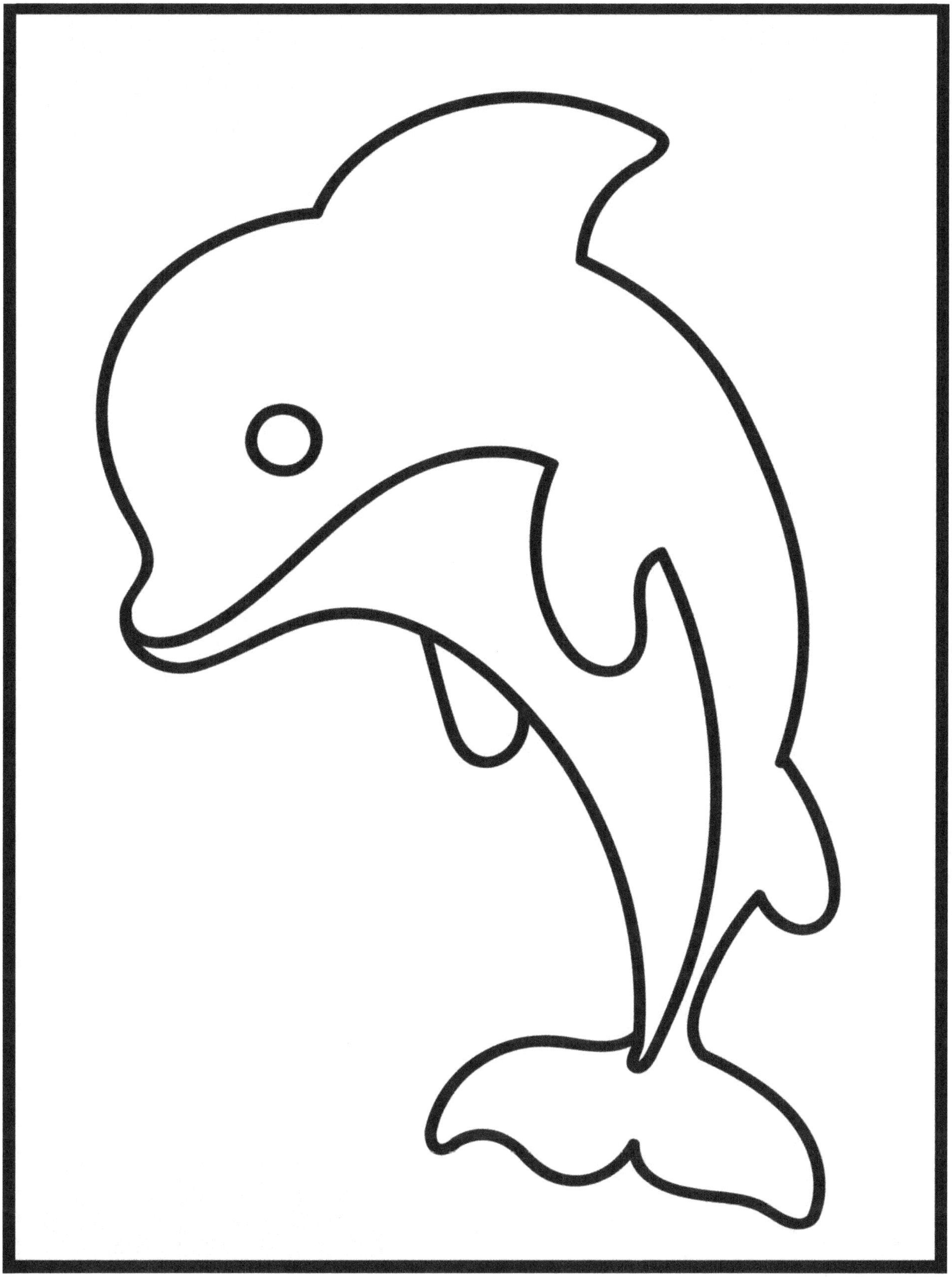

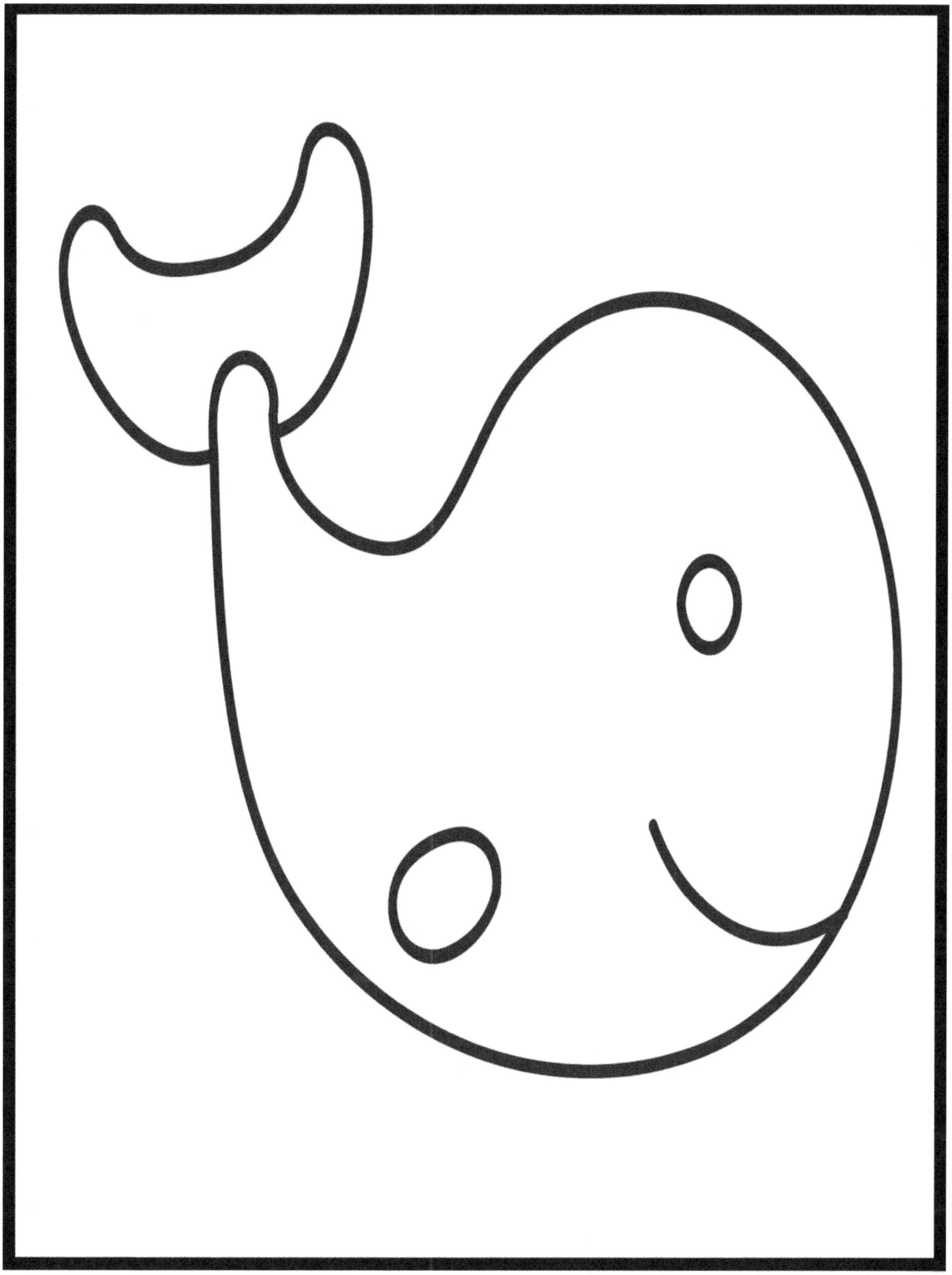

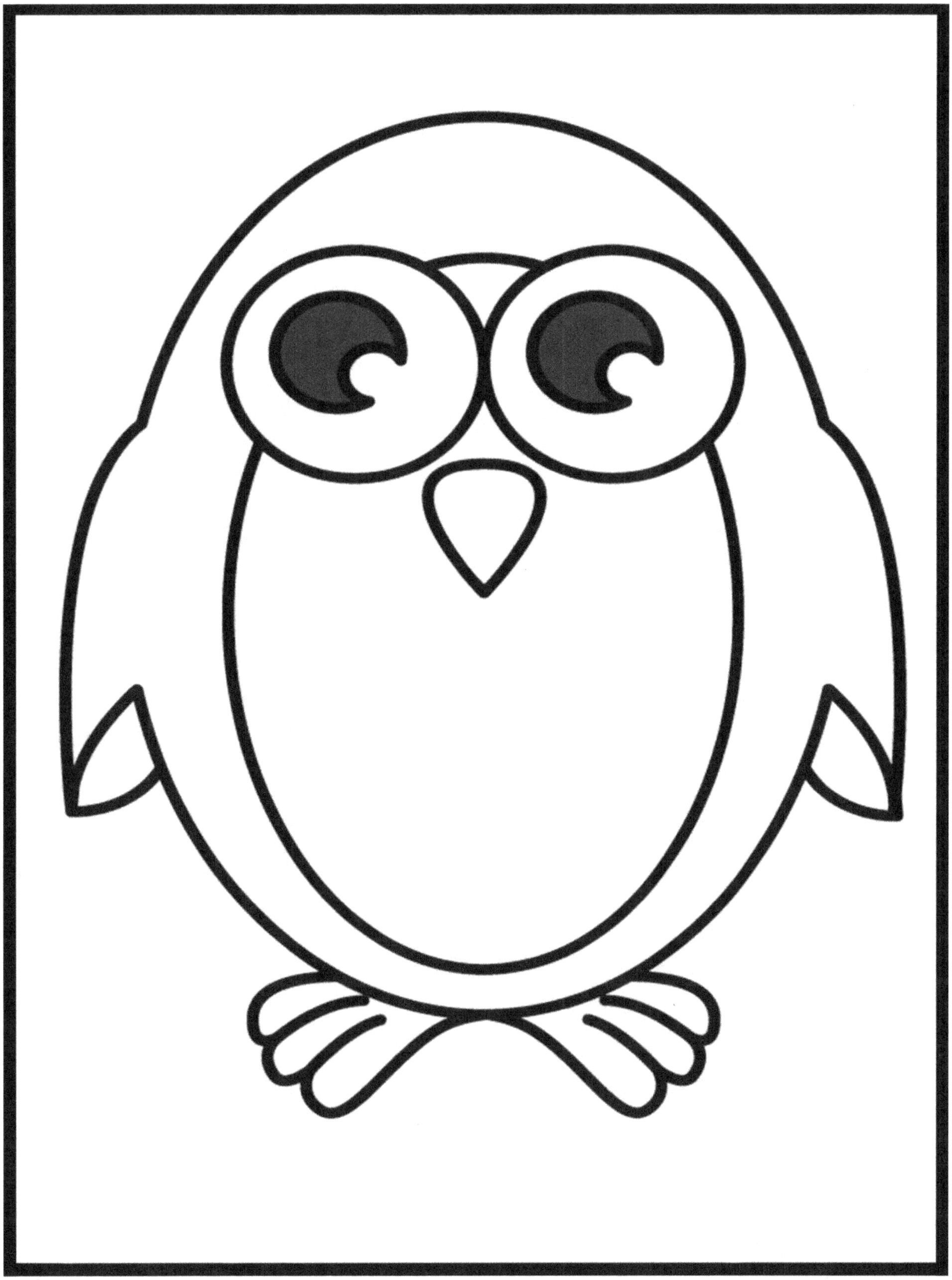

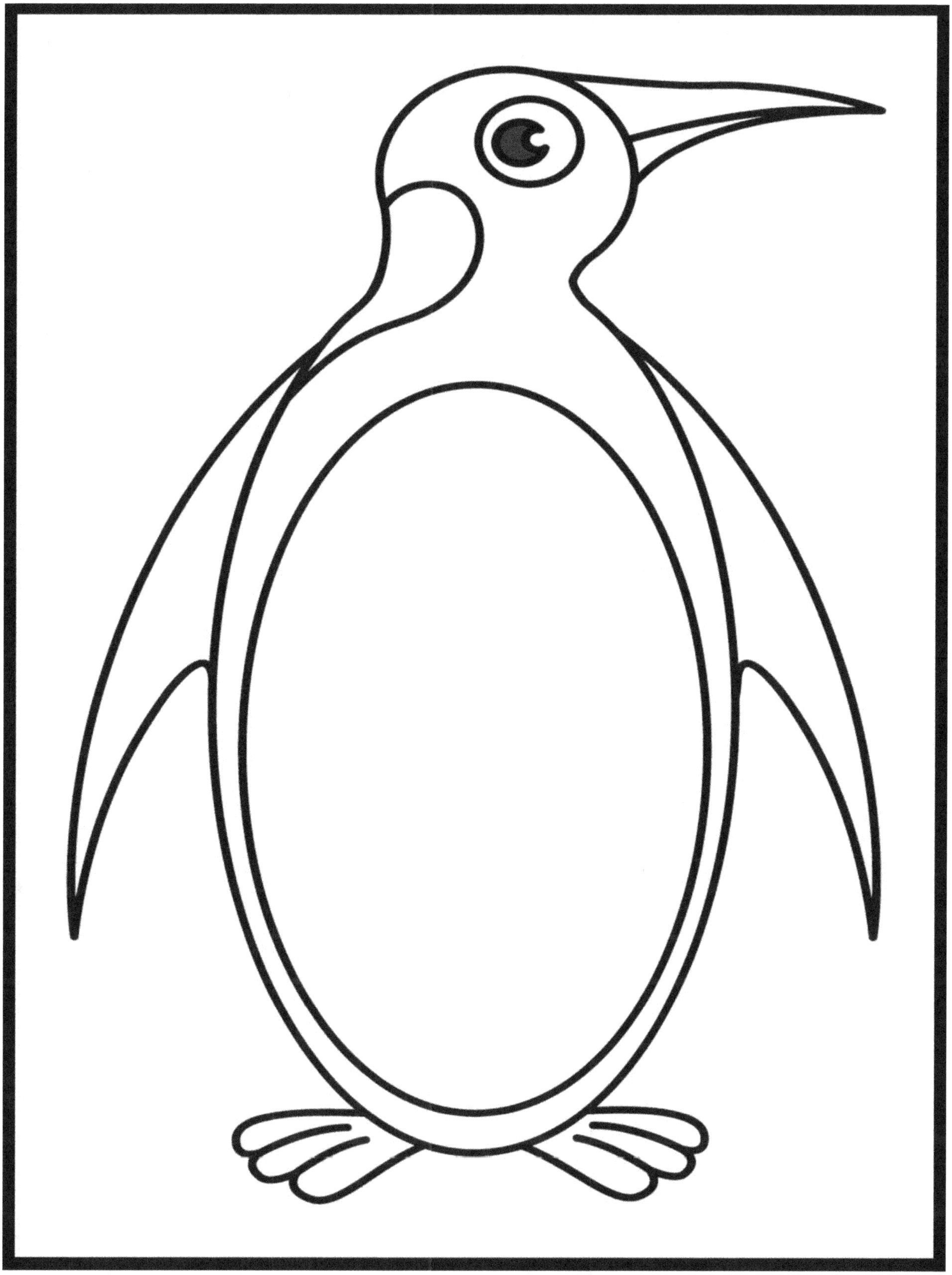

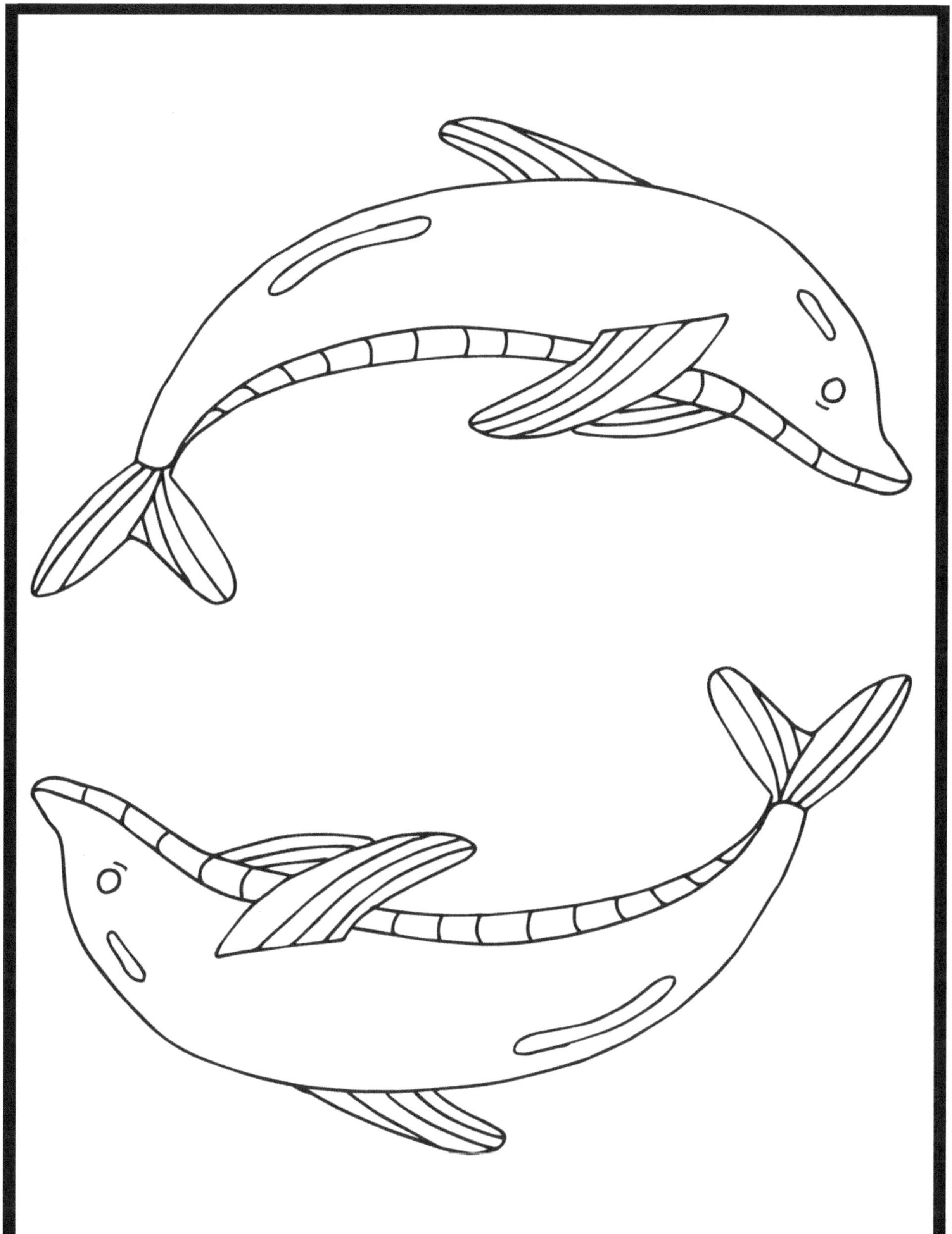

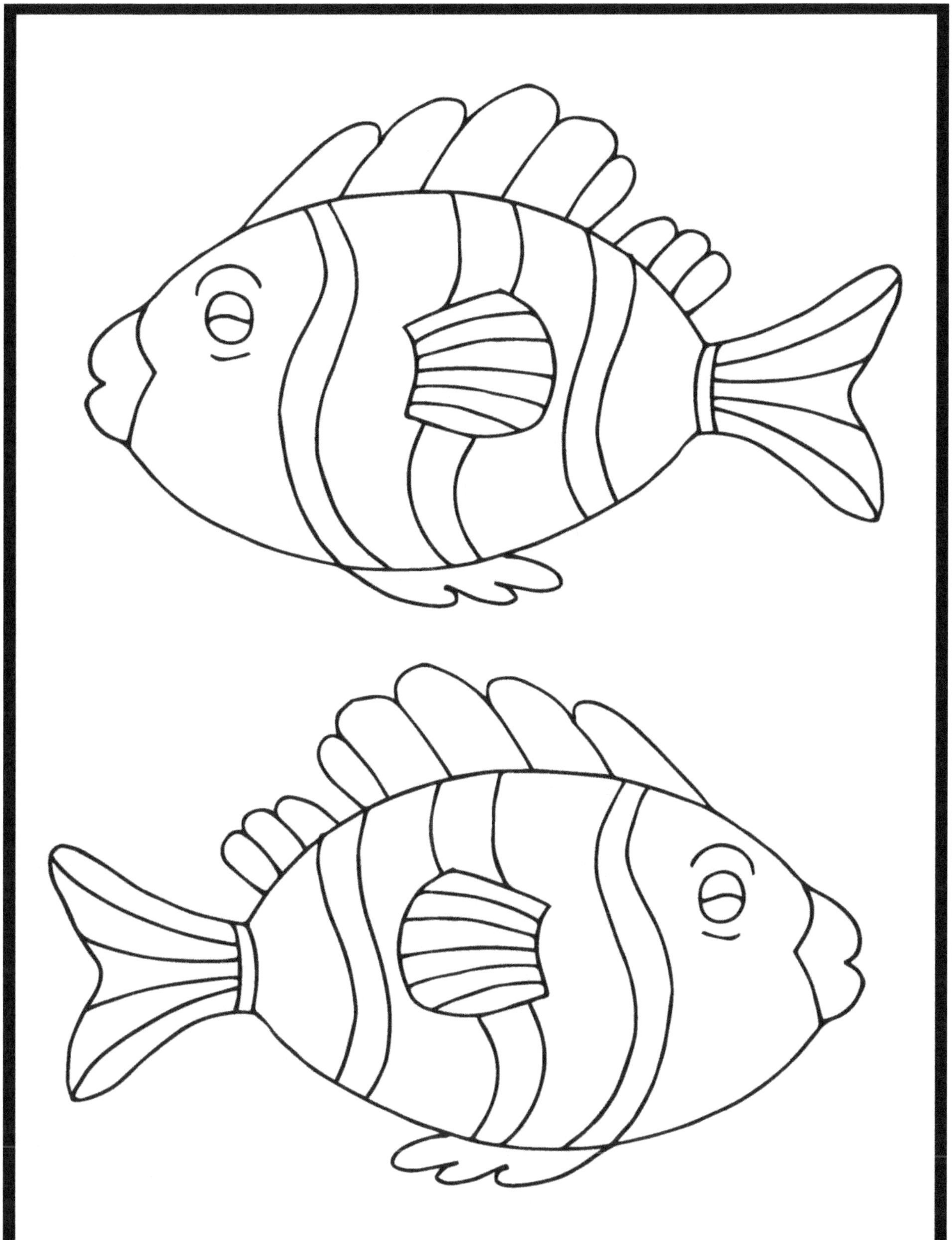

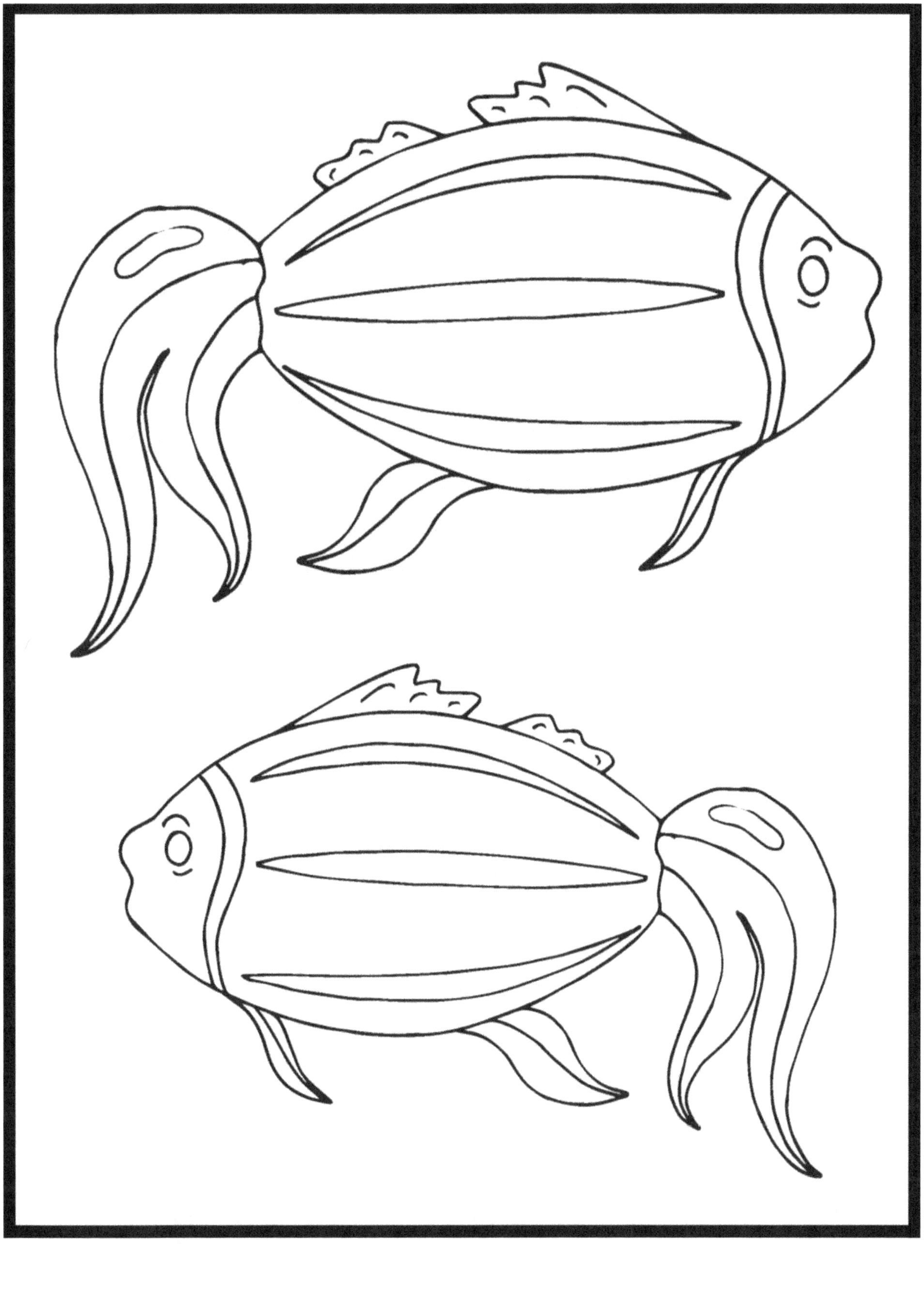

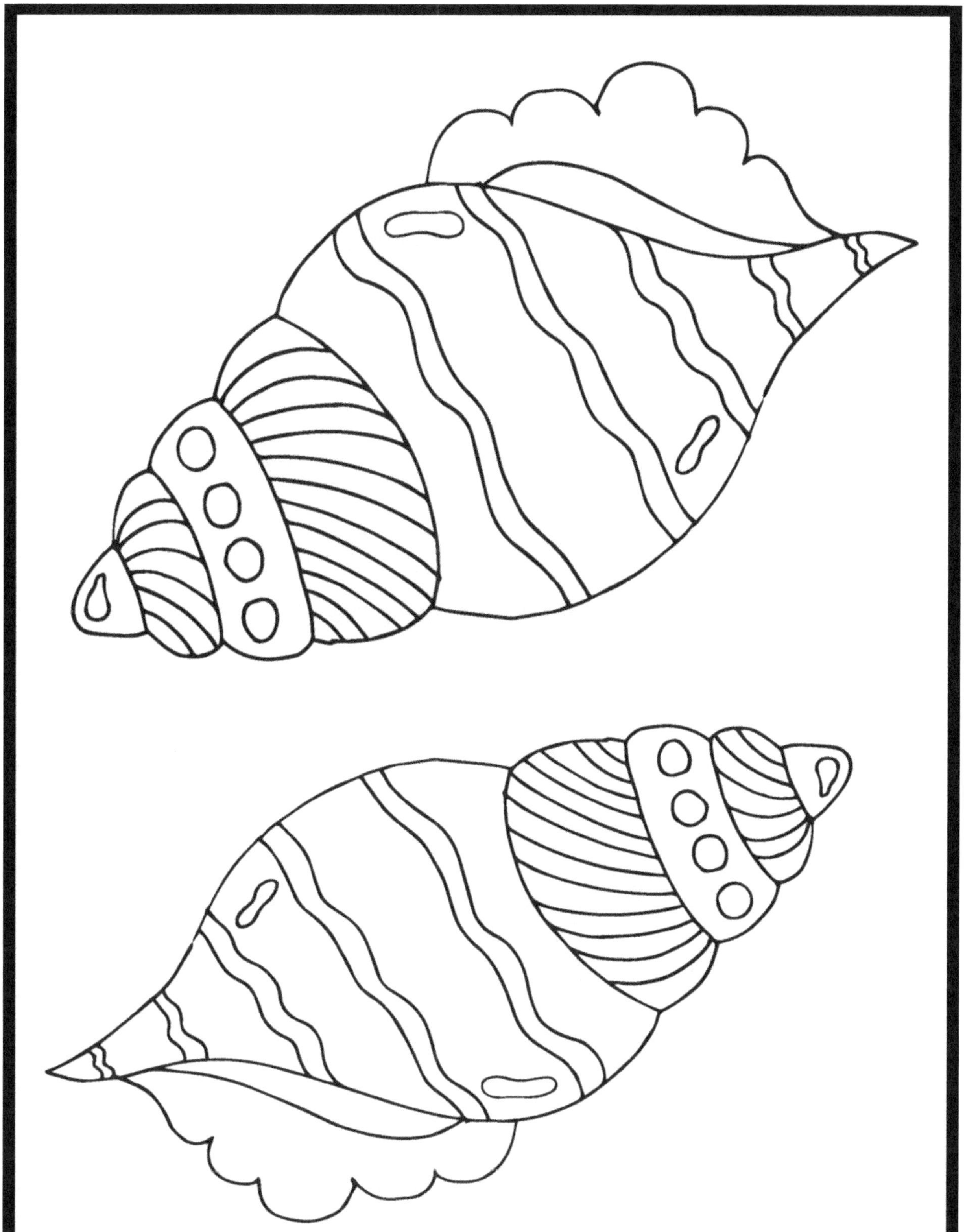

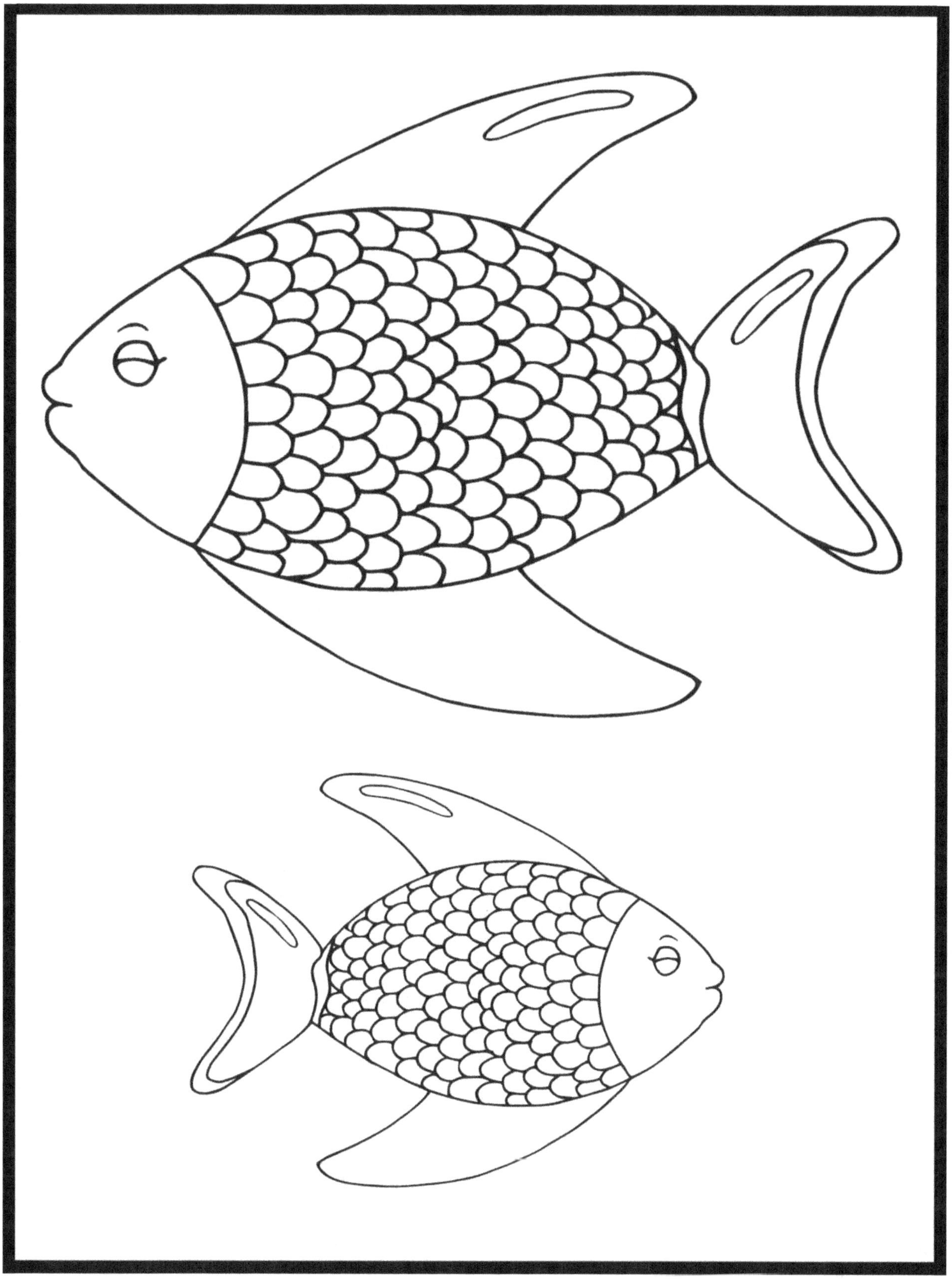

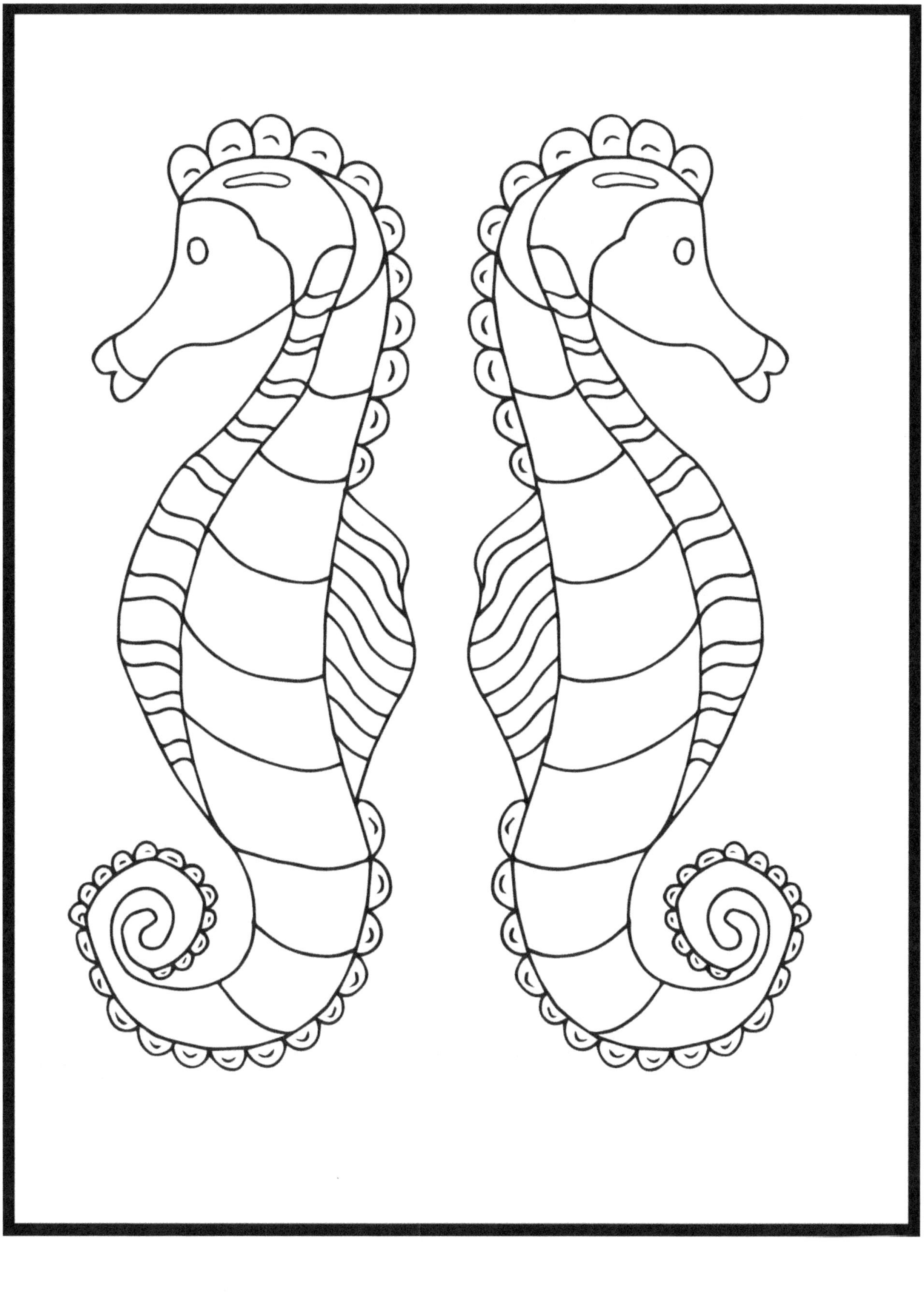

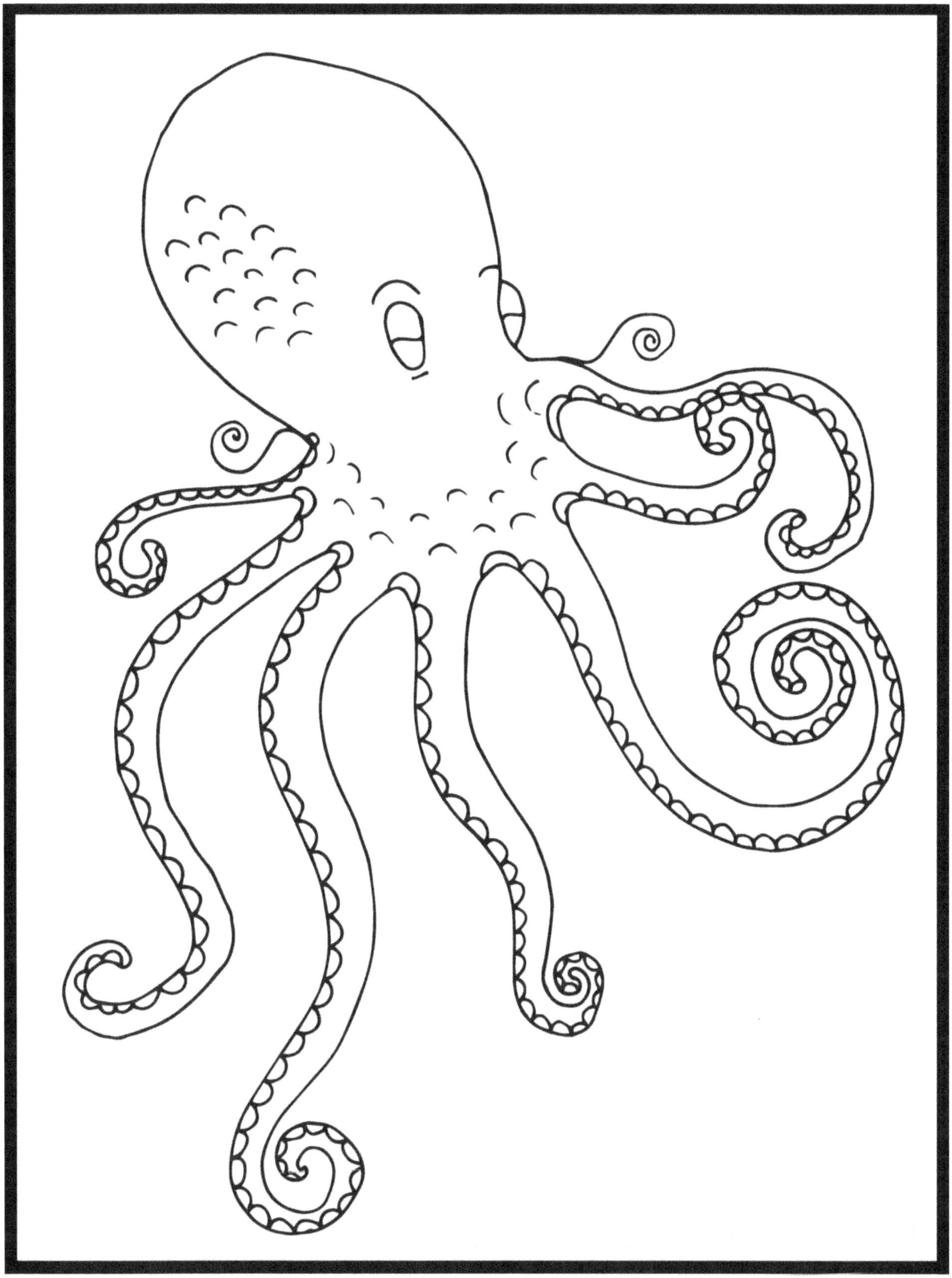

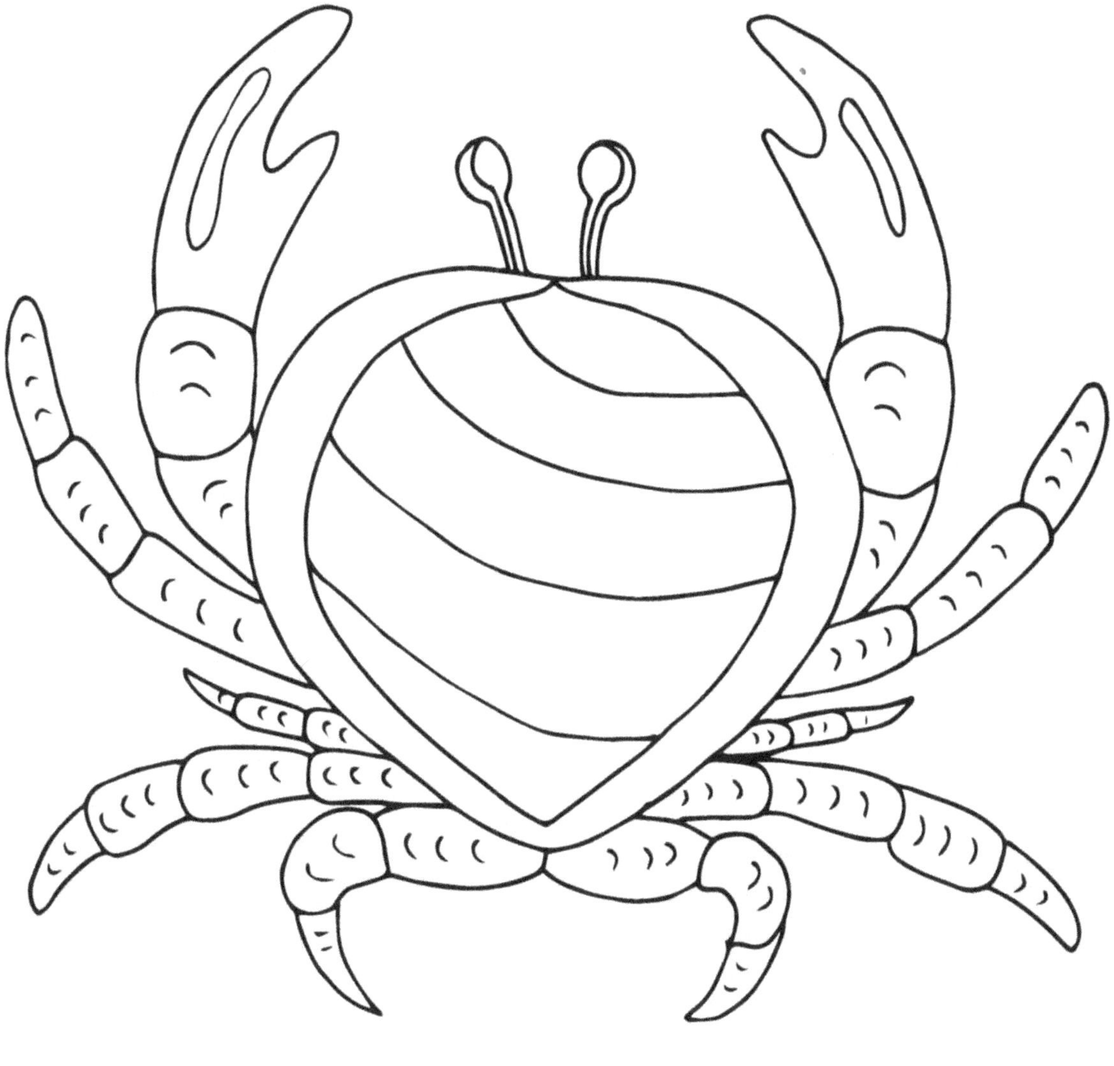

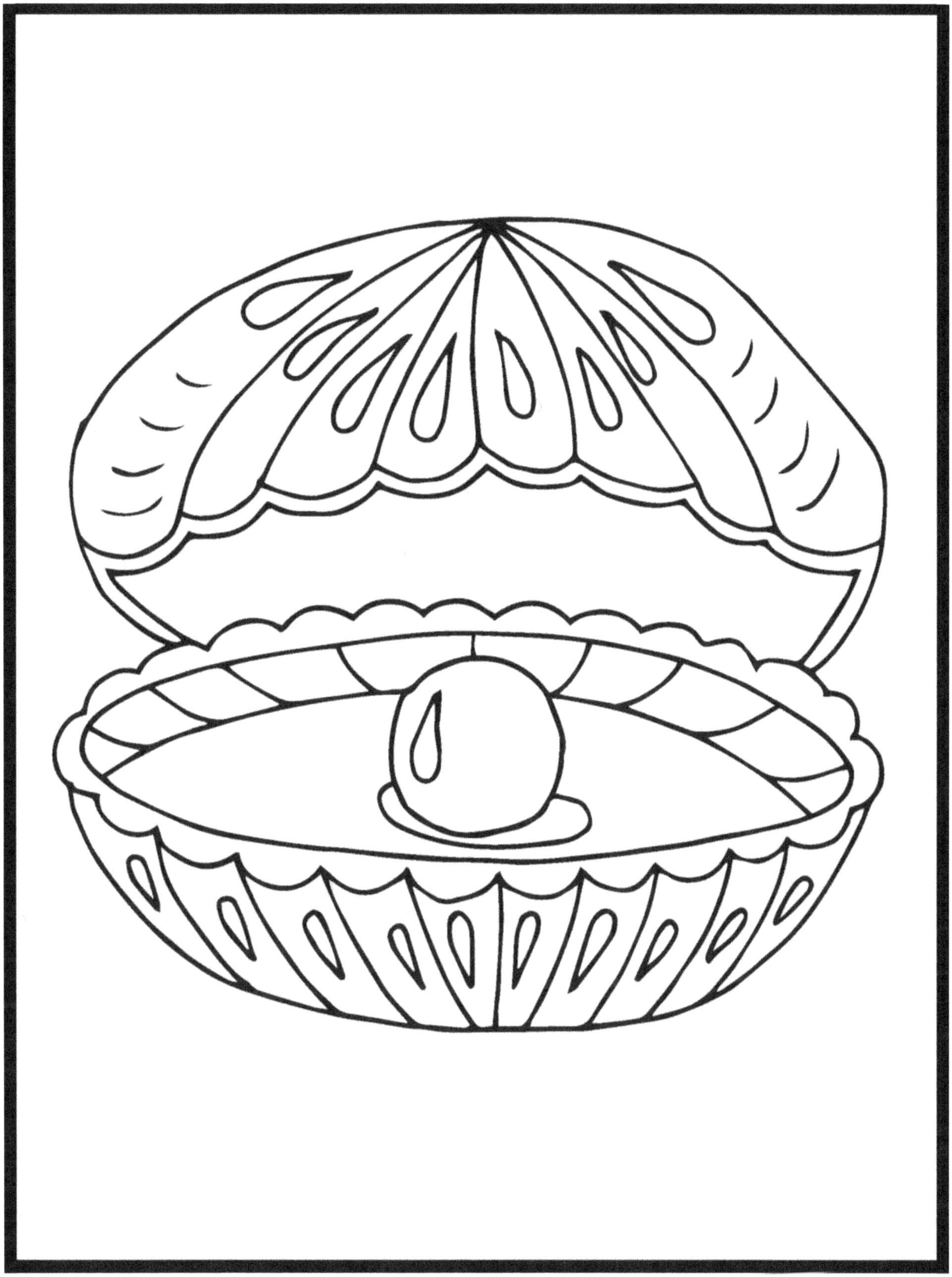

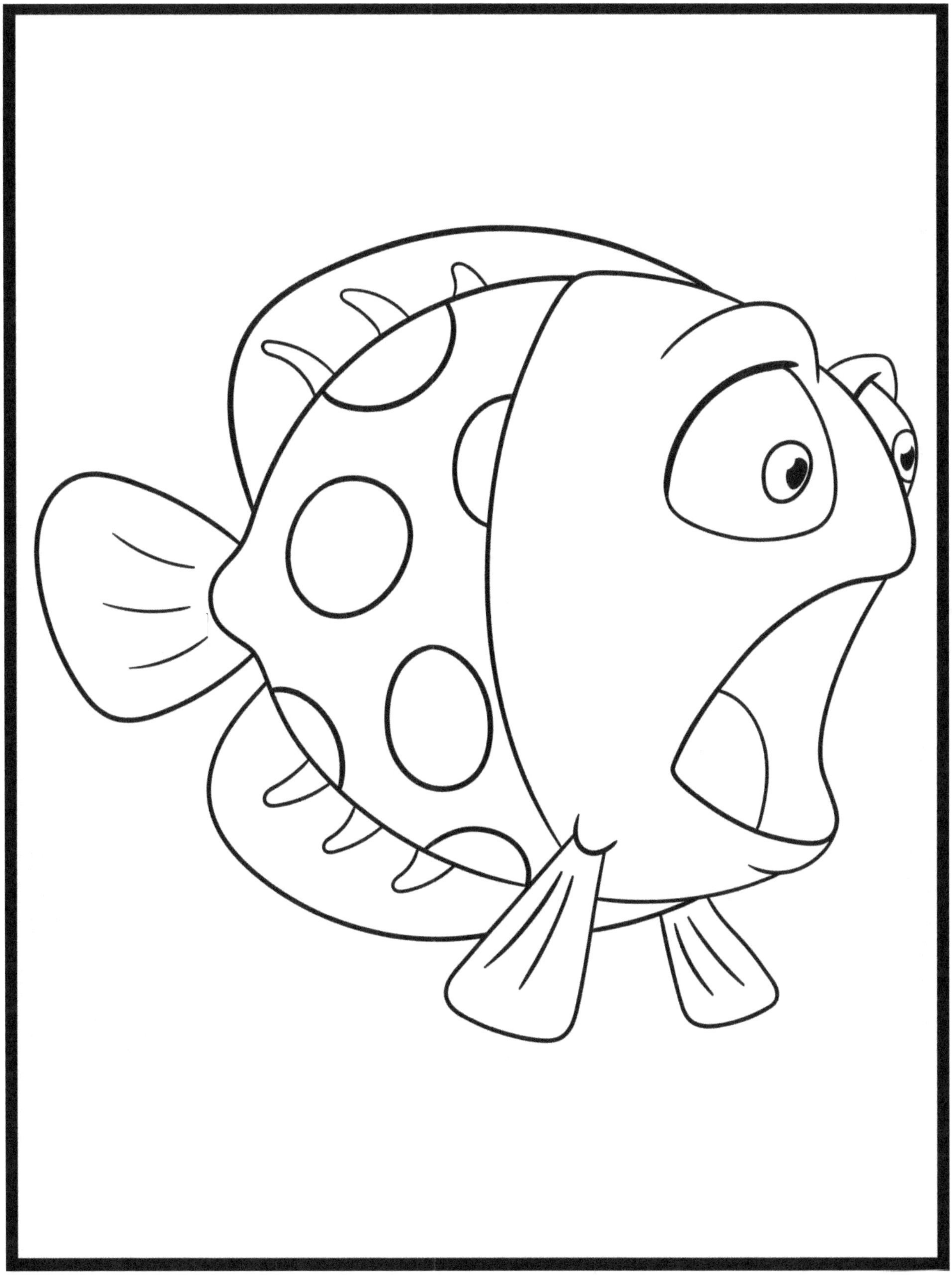

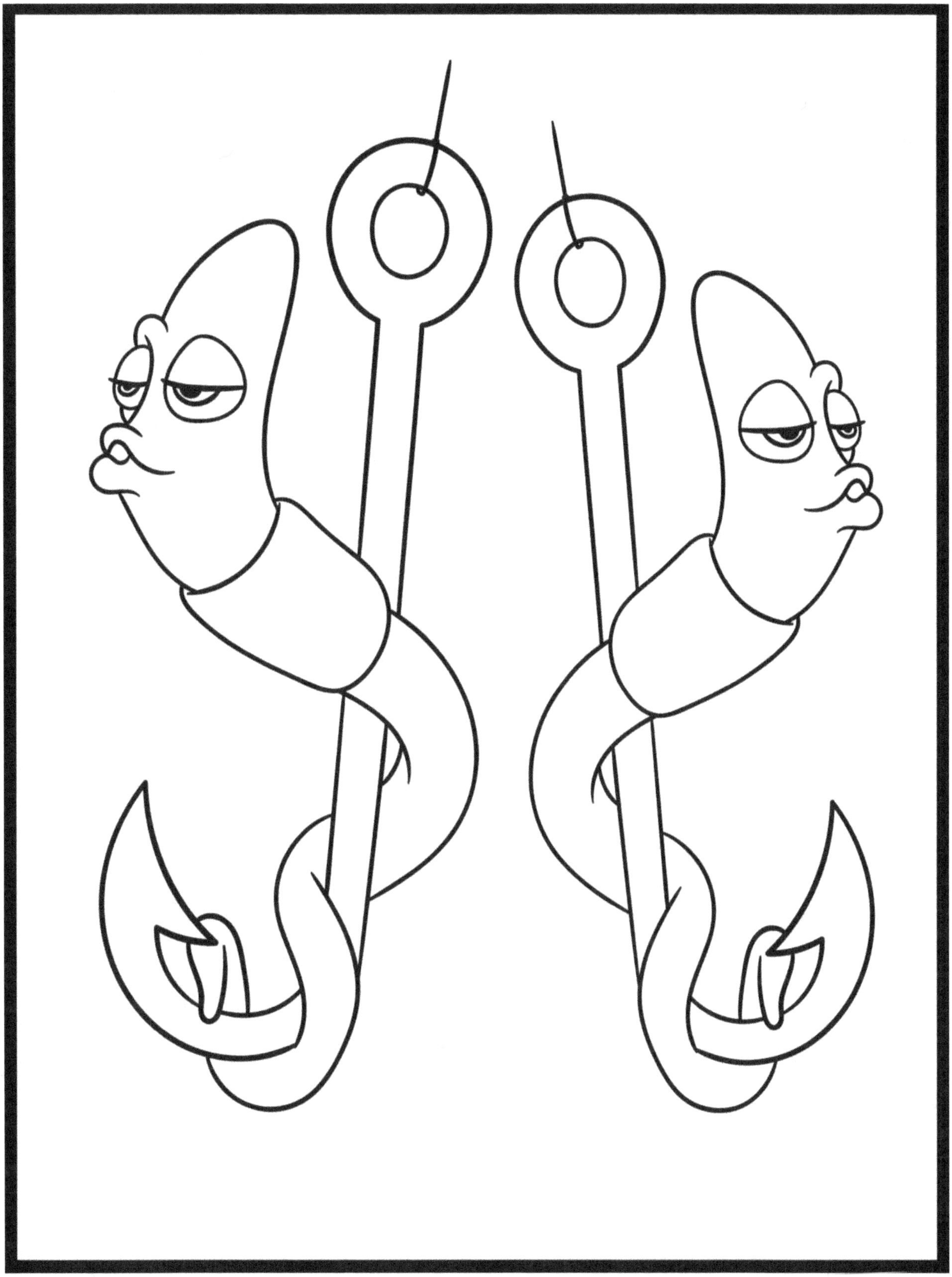

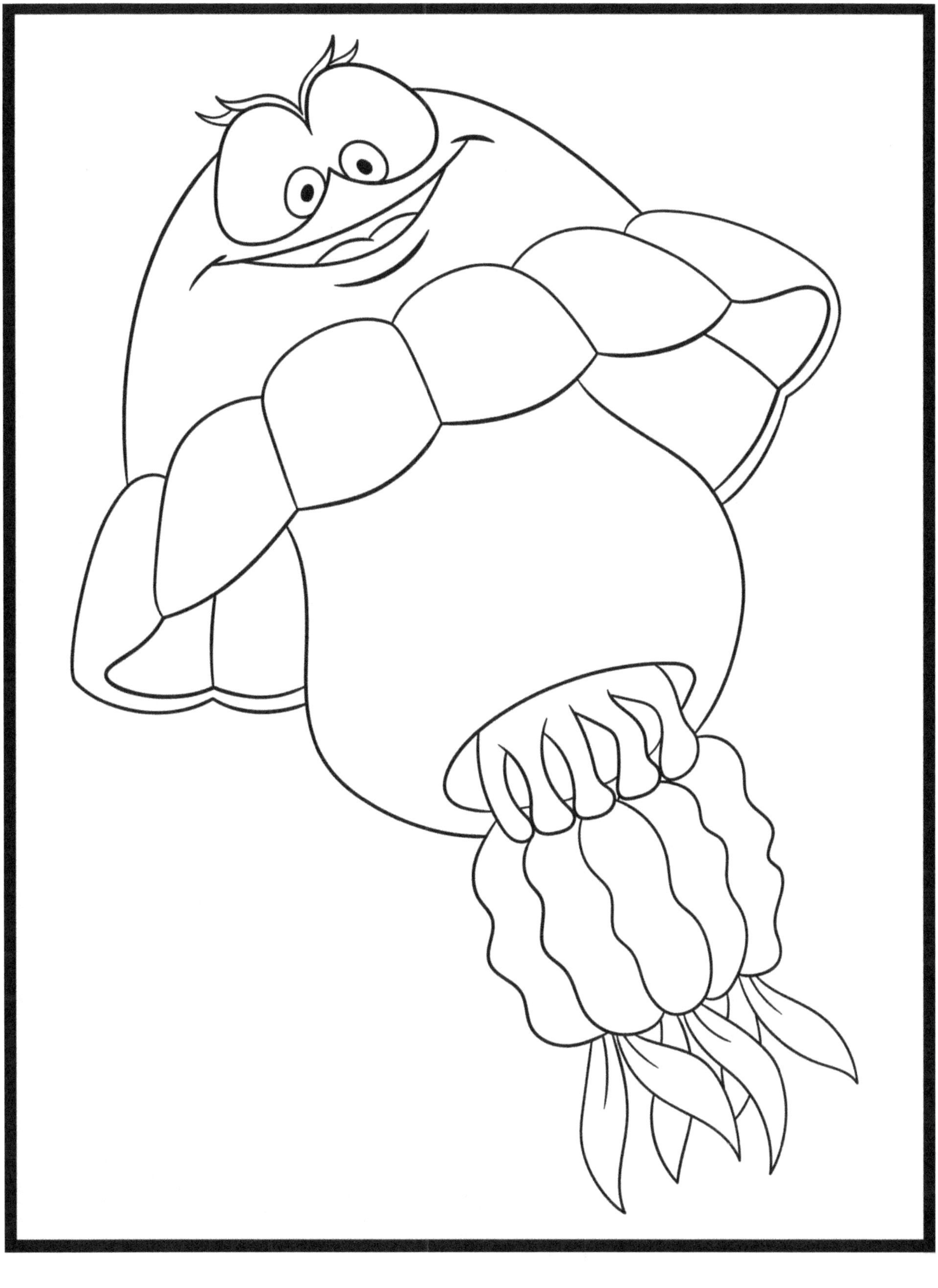

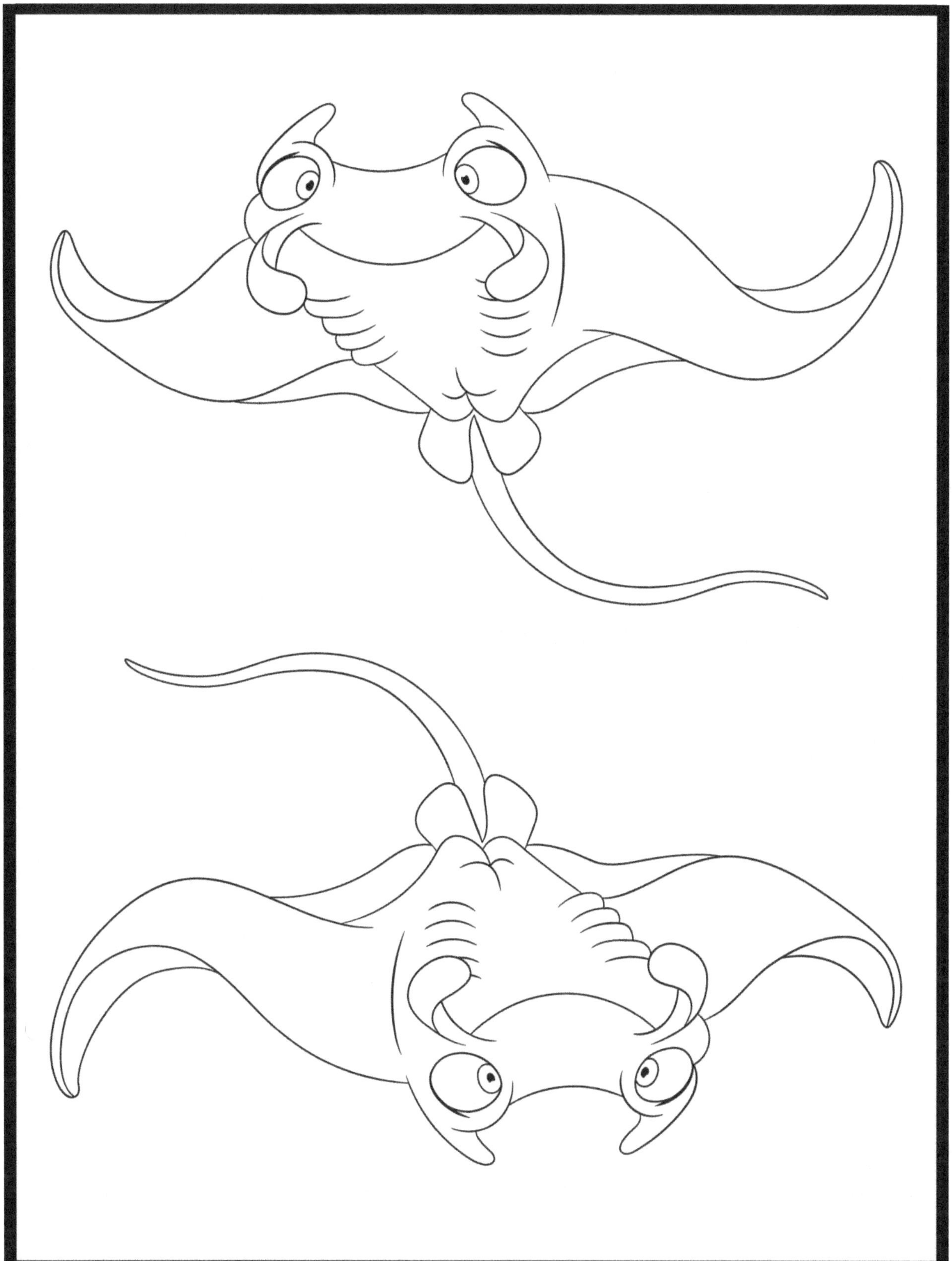

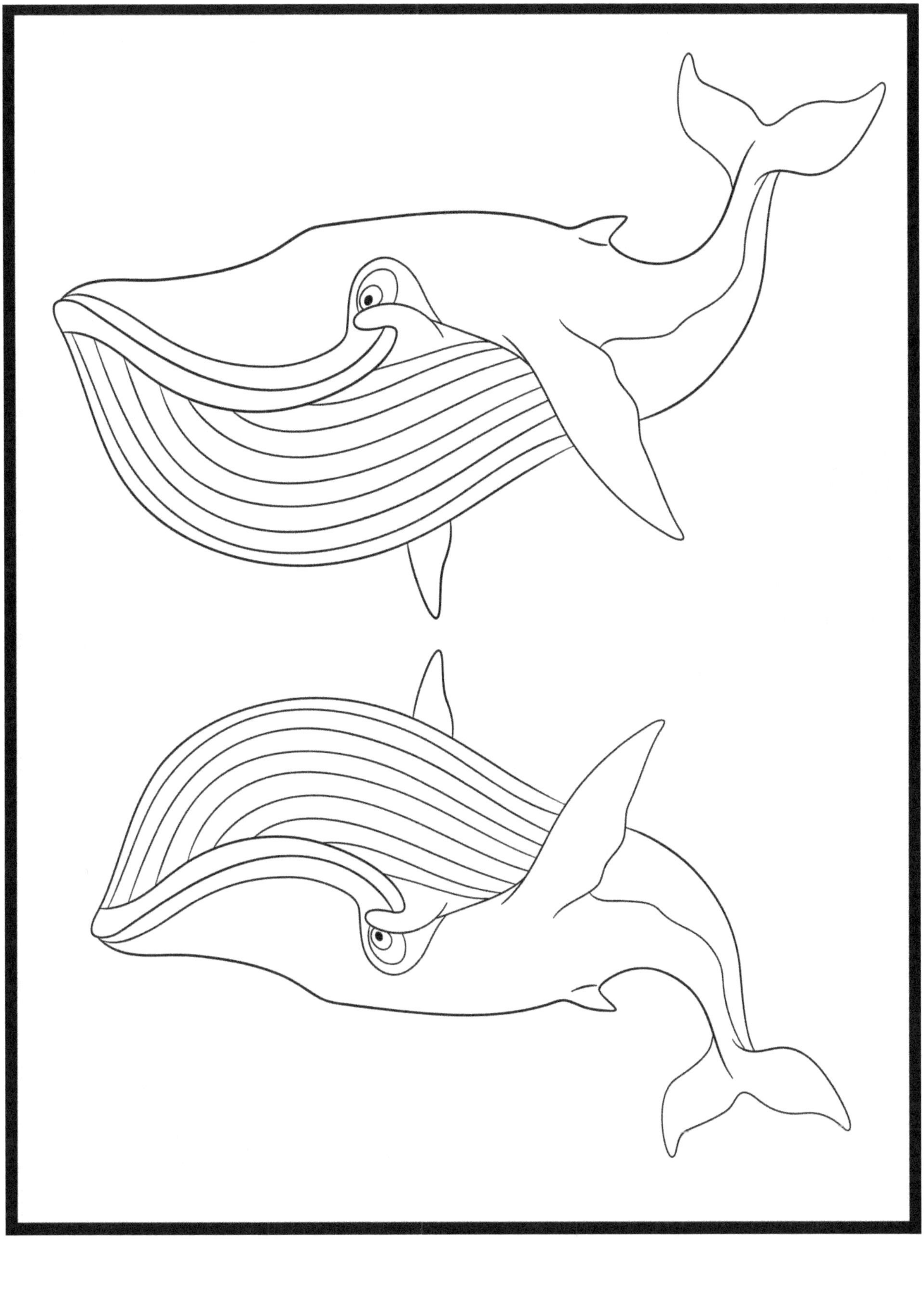

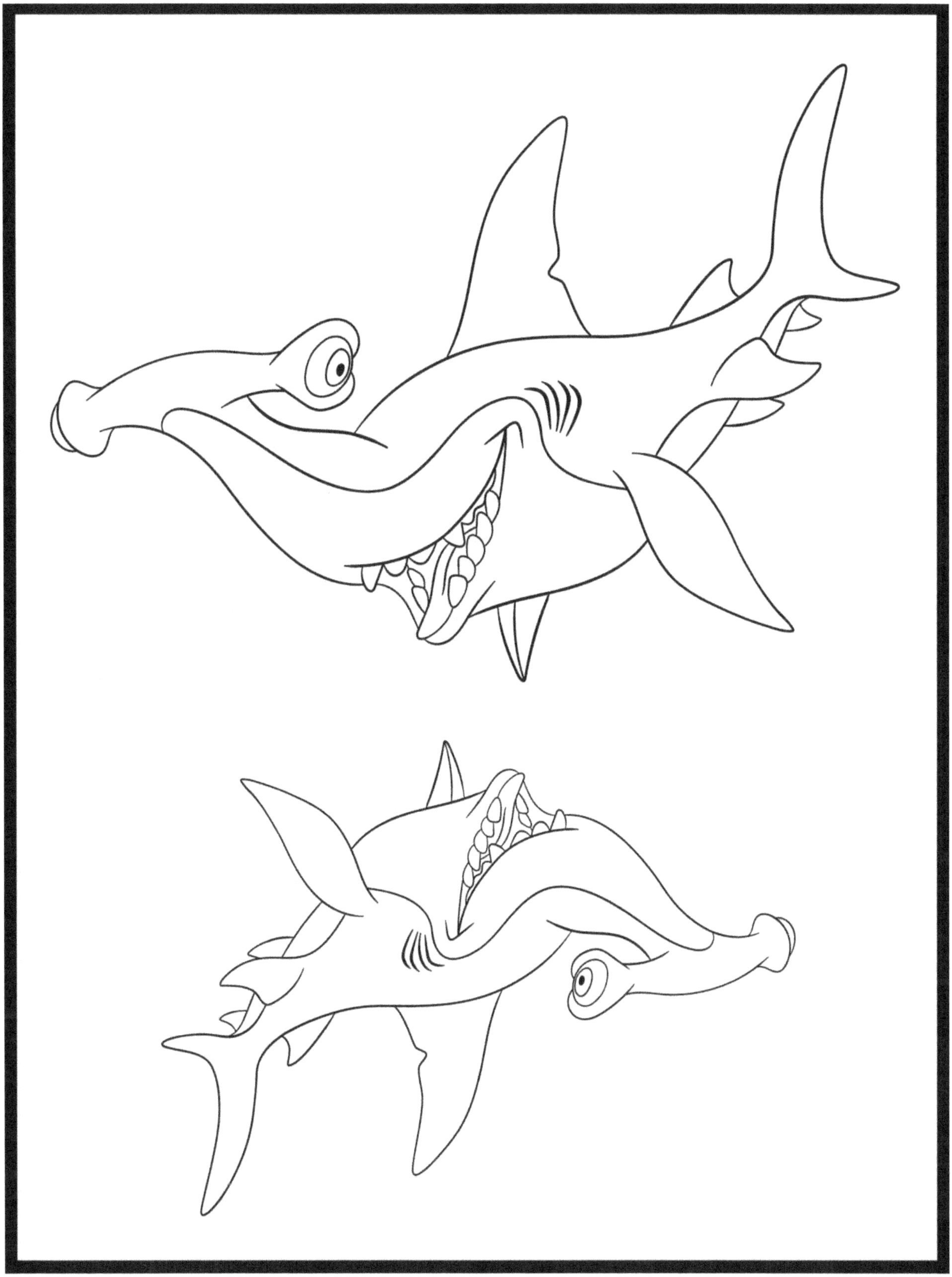

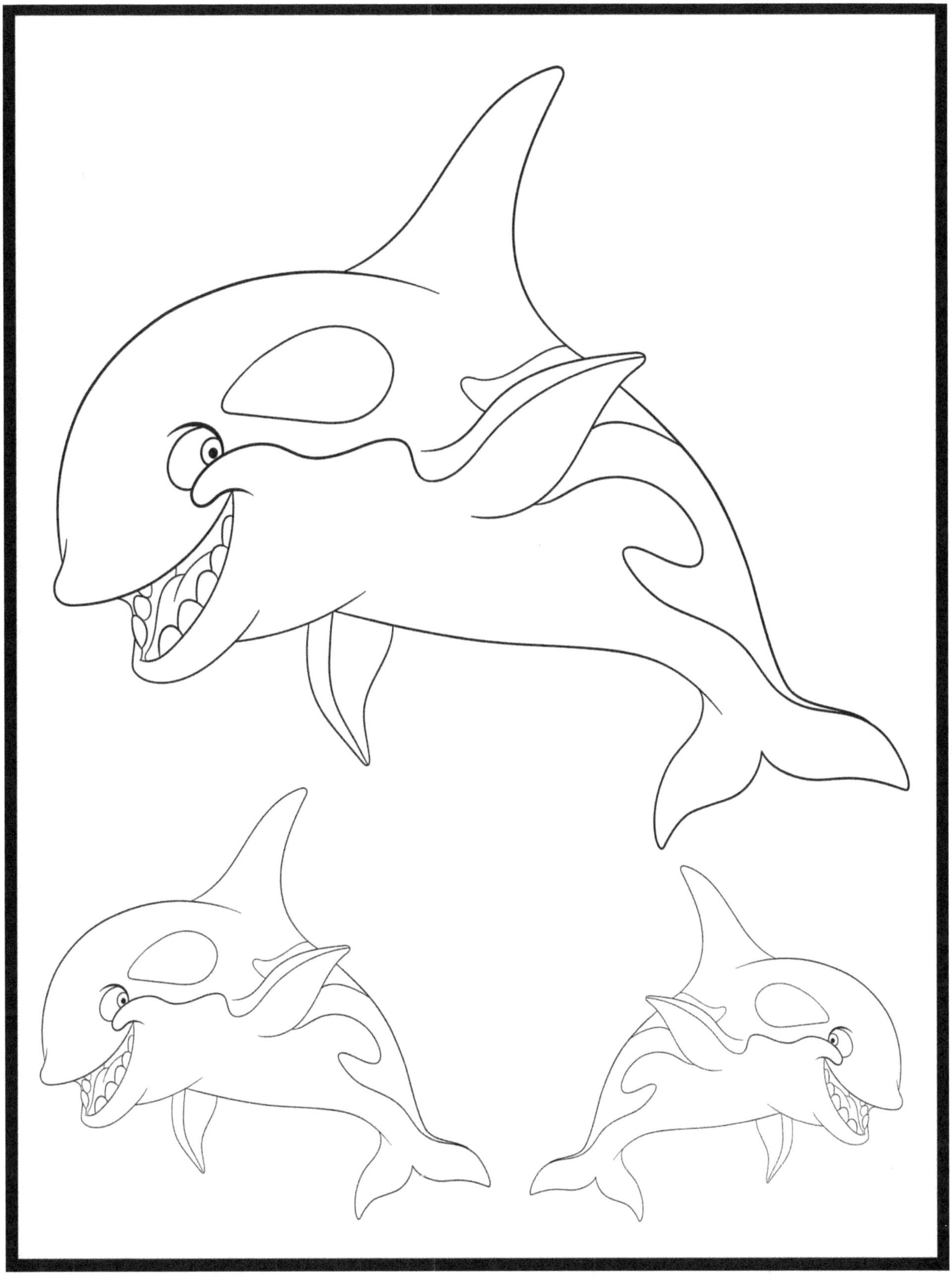

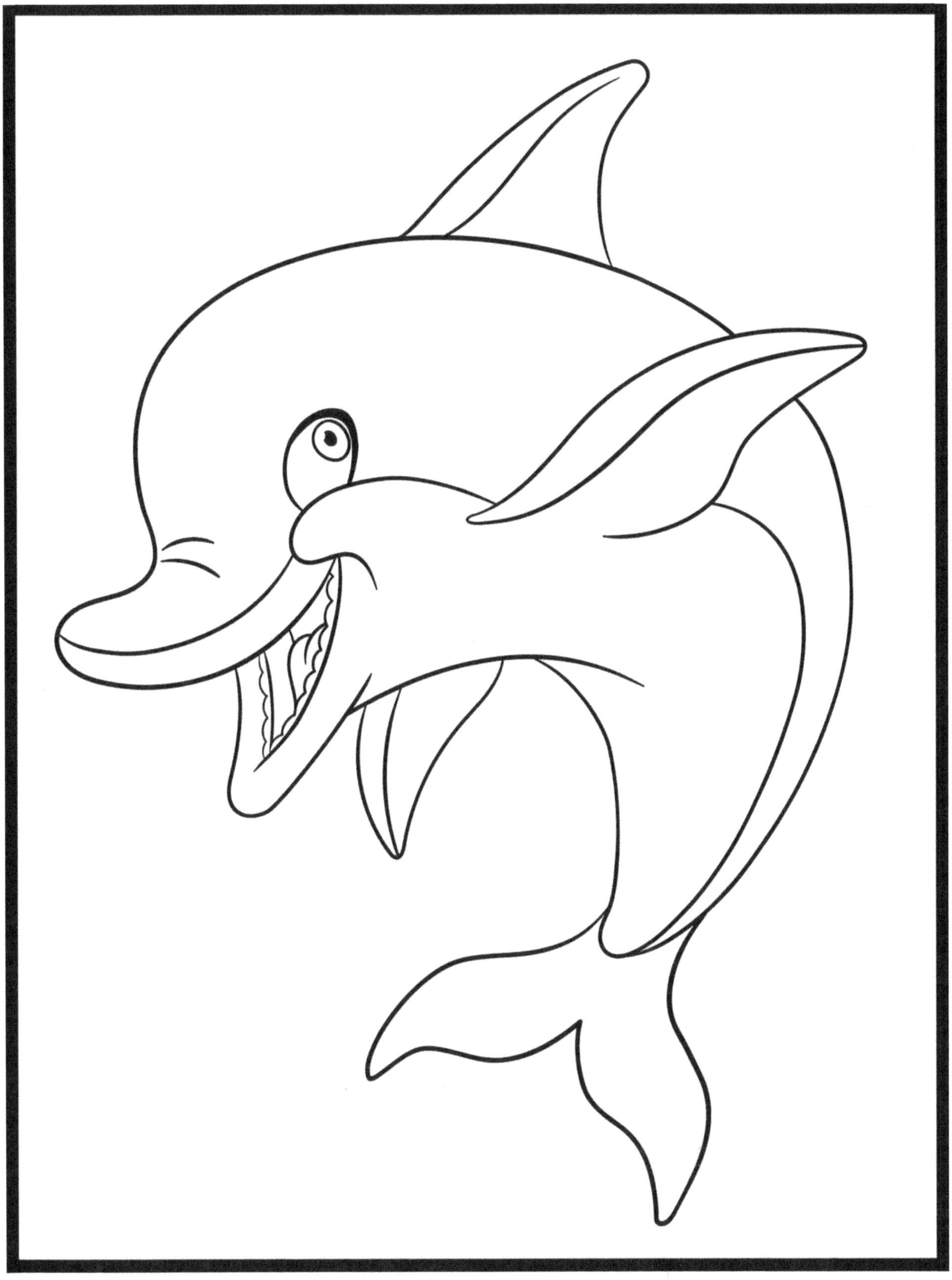

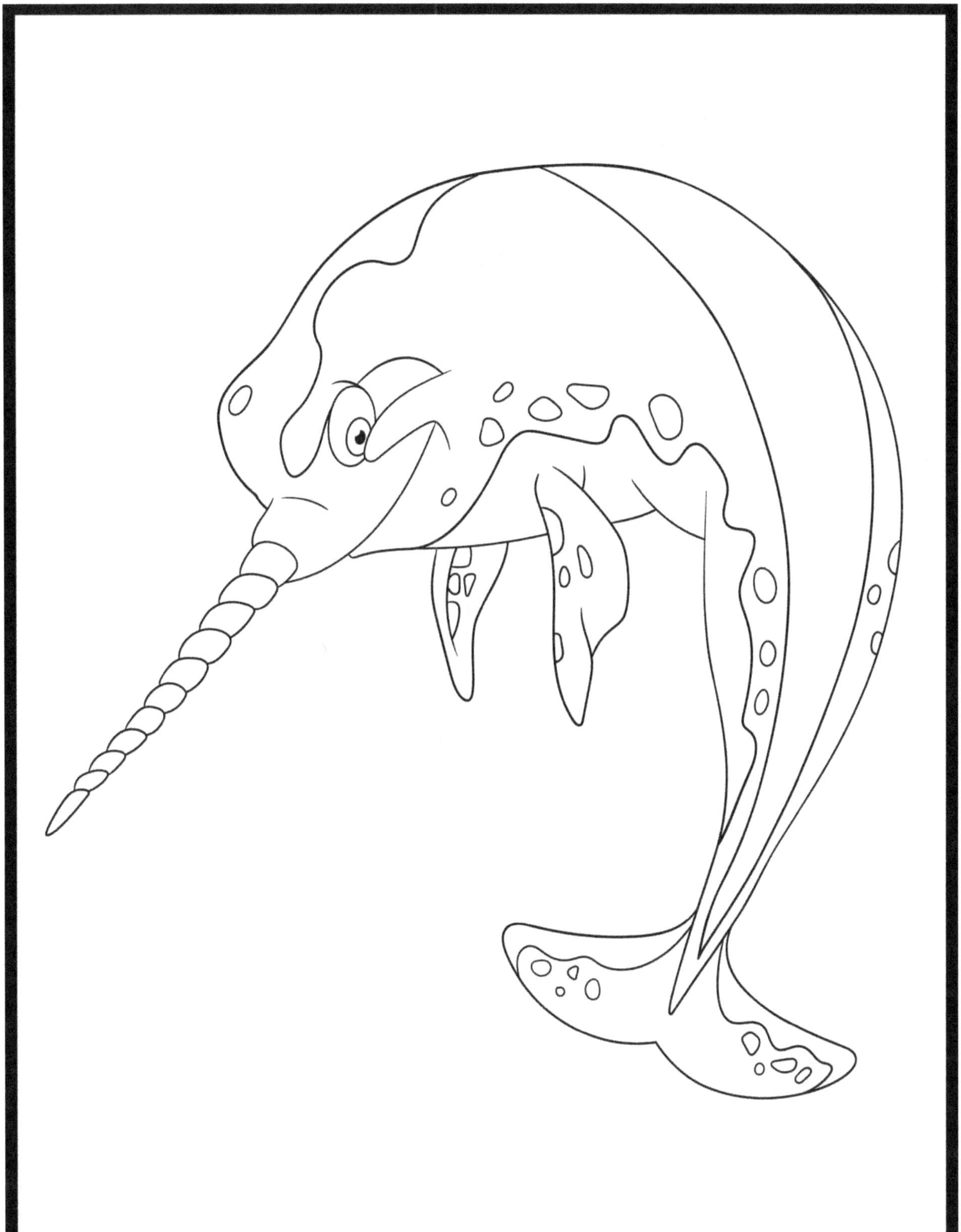

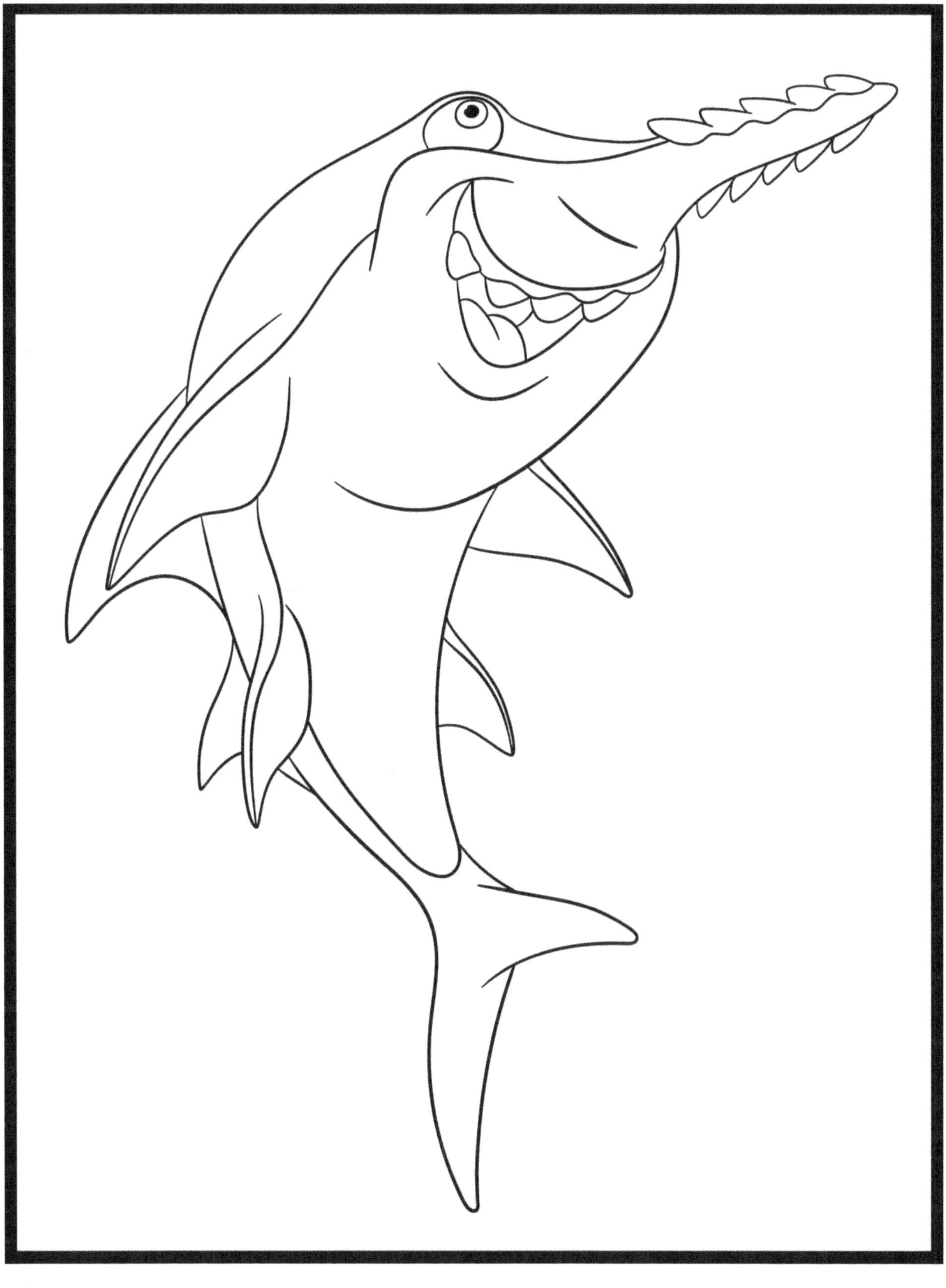

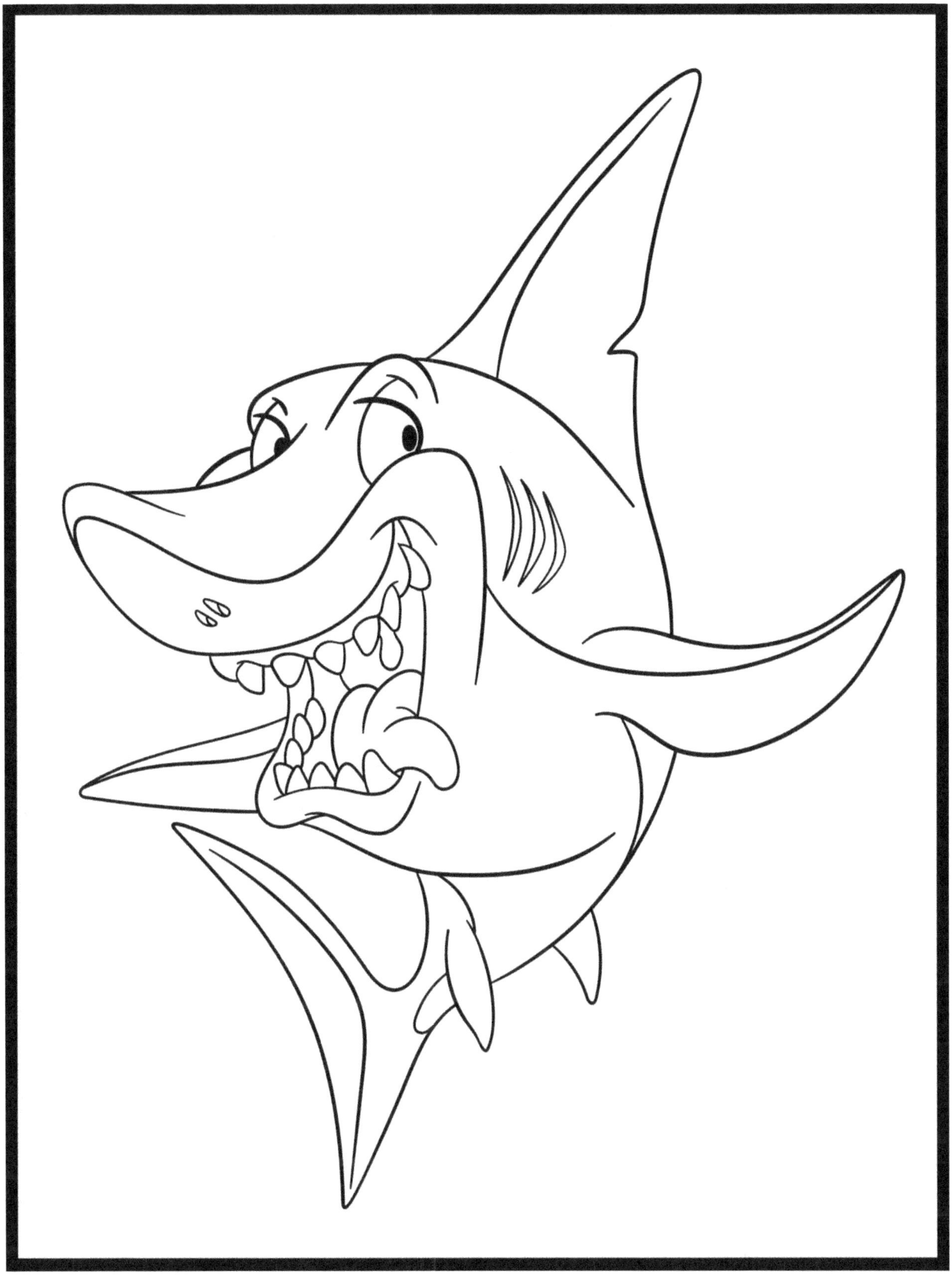

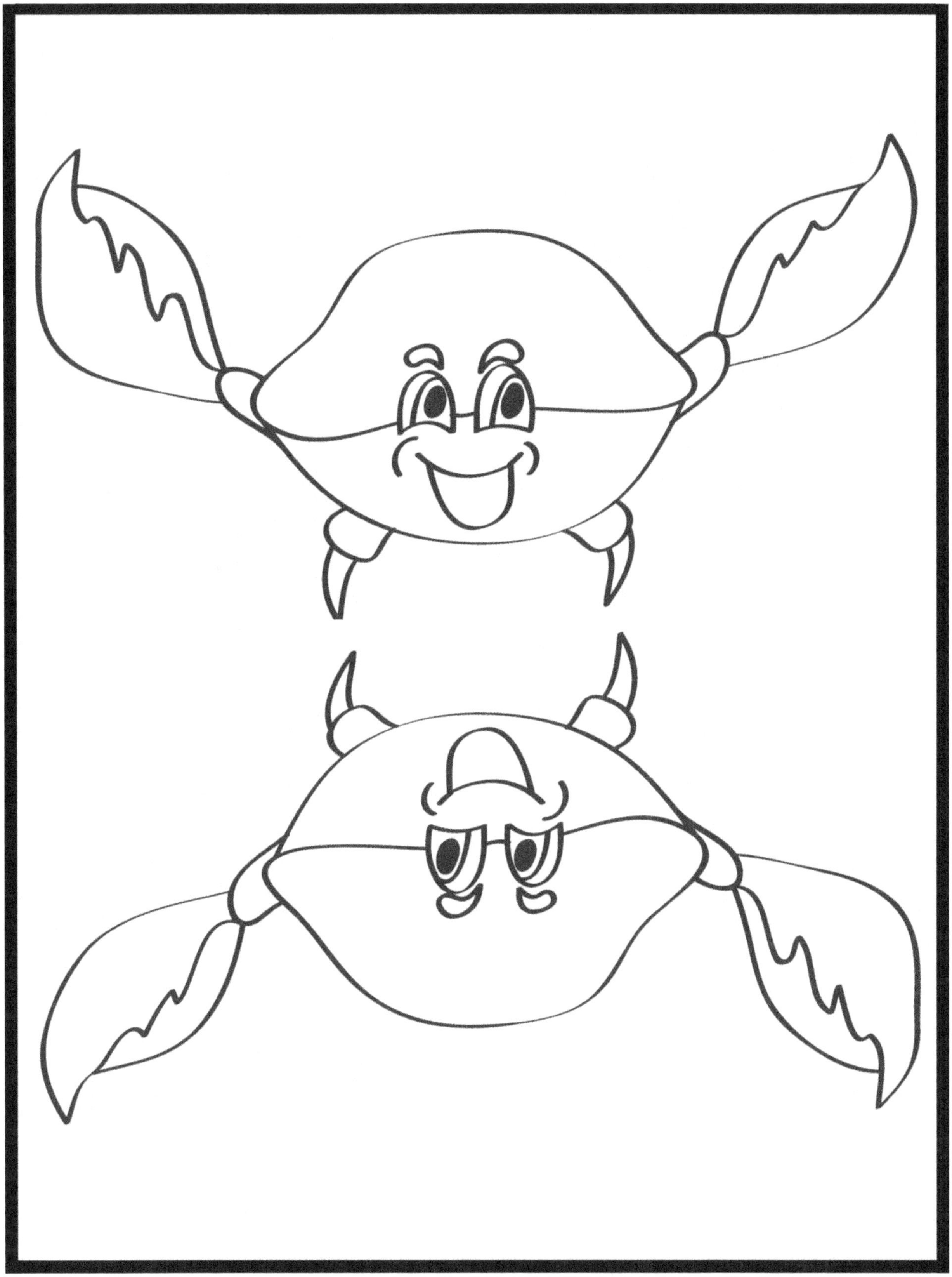

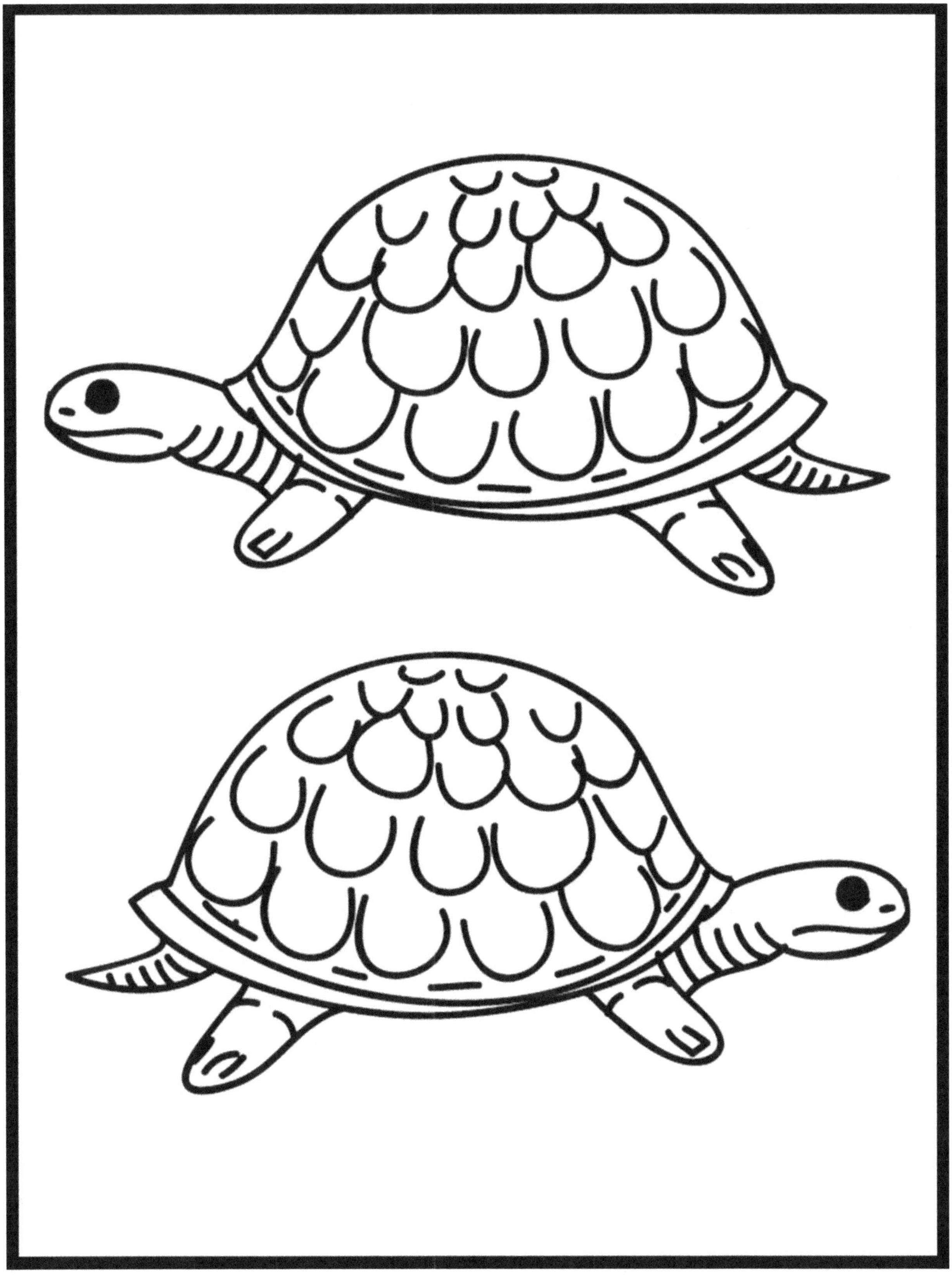

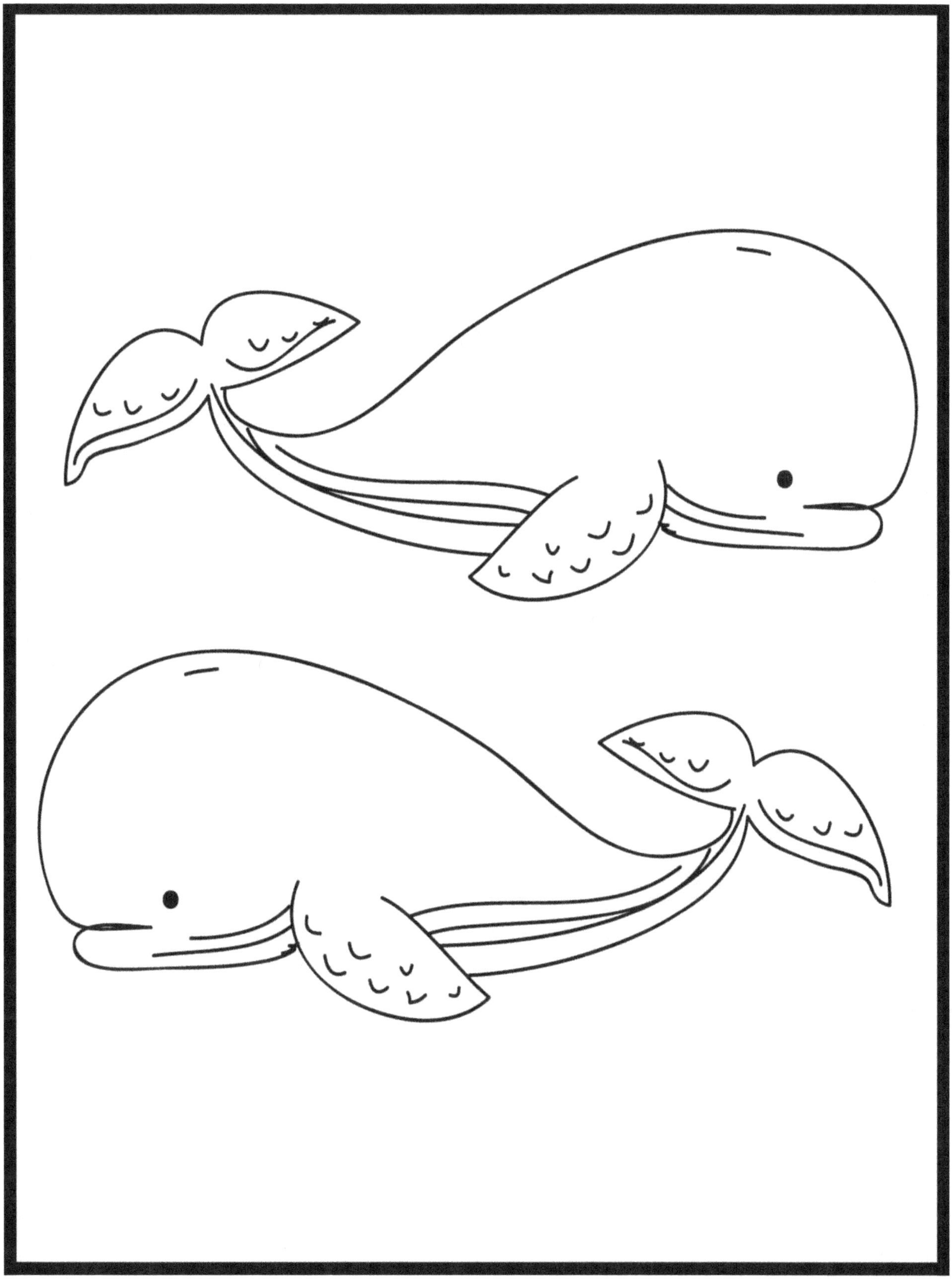

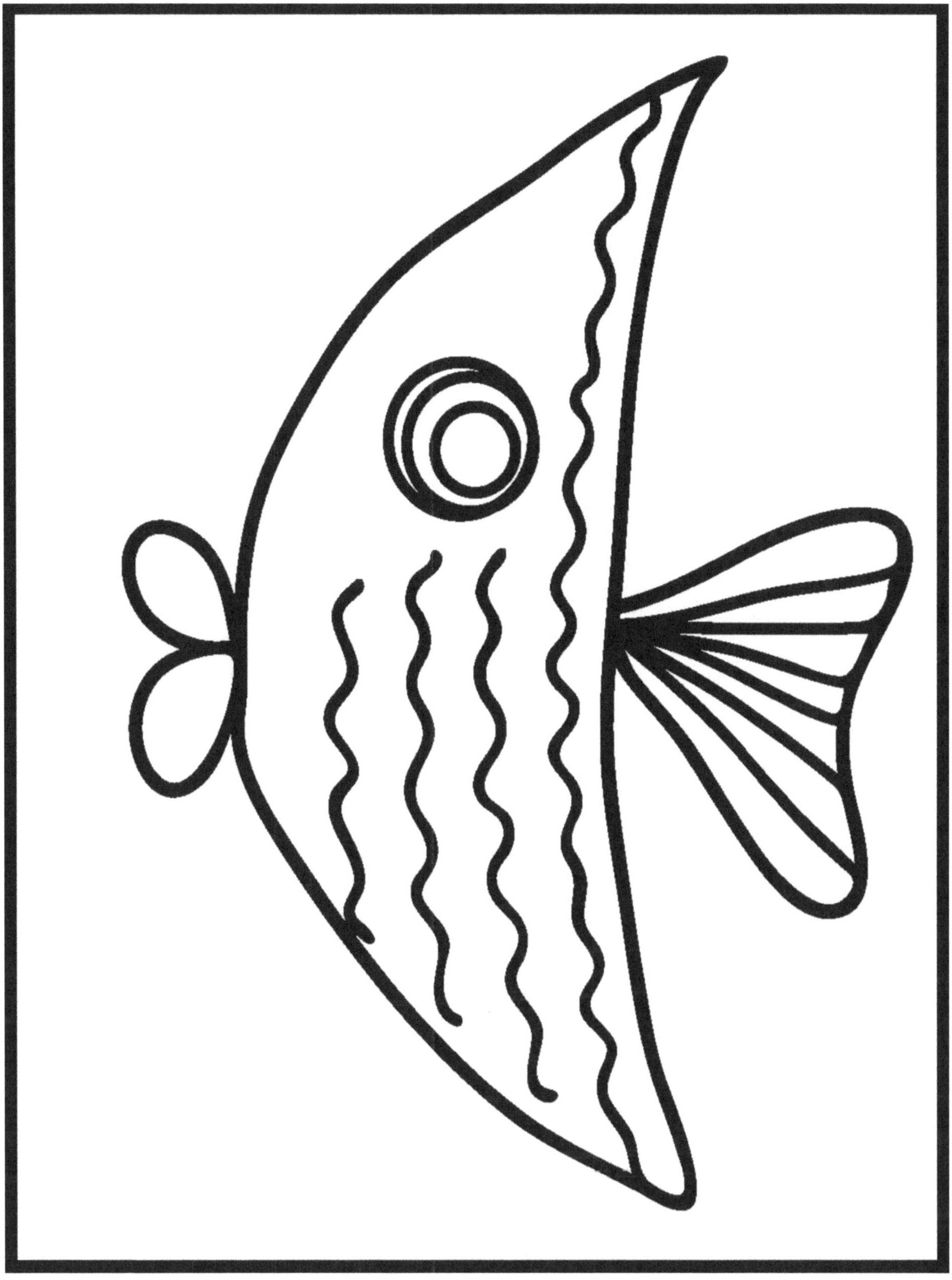

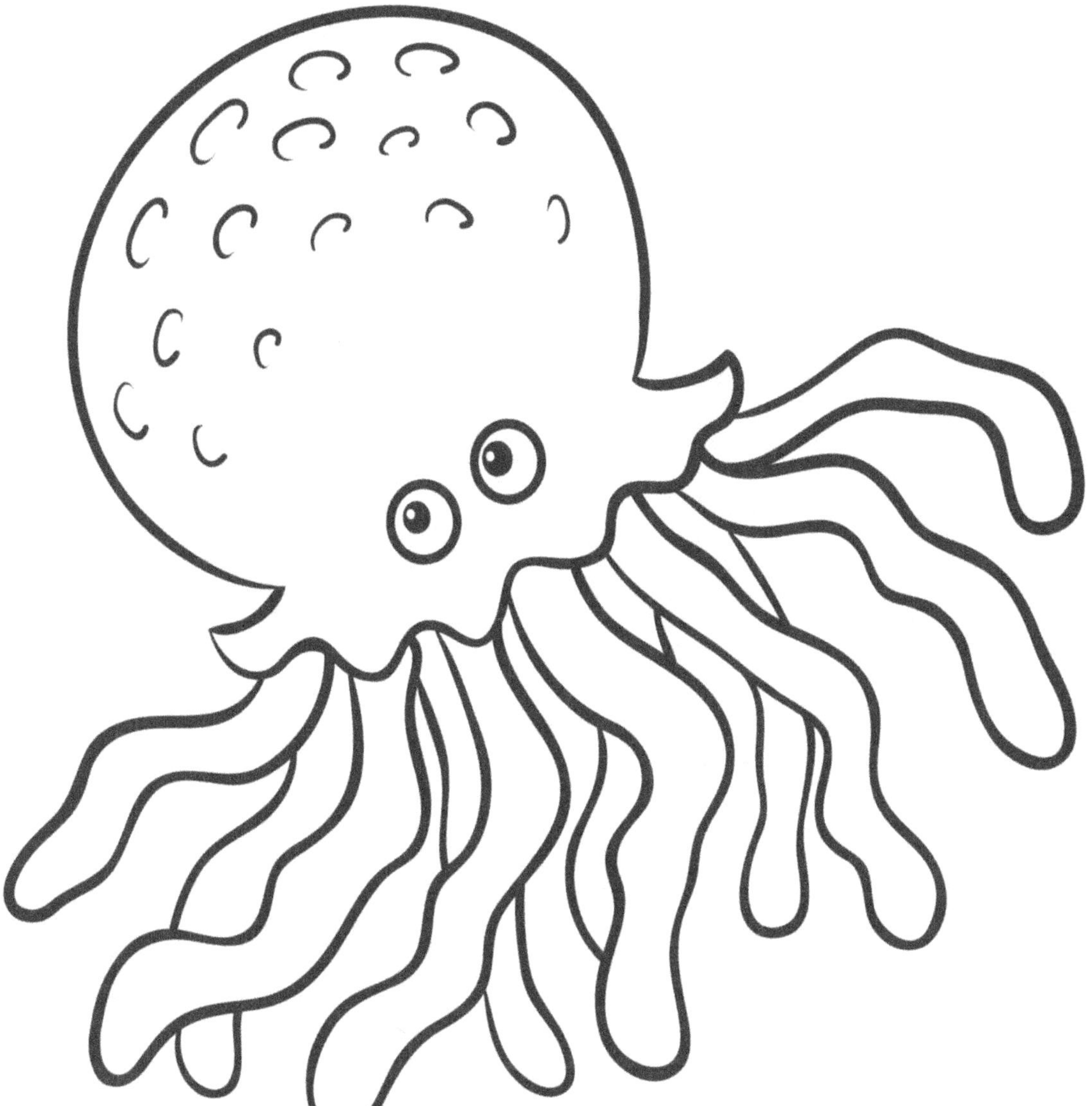

www.ingramcontent.com/pod-product-compliance
Lightning Source LLC
Chambersburg PA
CBHW082114220526
45472CB00009B/2176
* 9 7 8 1 7 2 0 3 4 6 0 6 7 *